Eyewitness
EARLY HUMANS

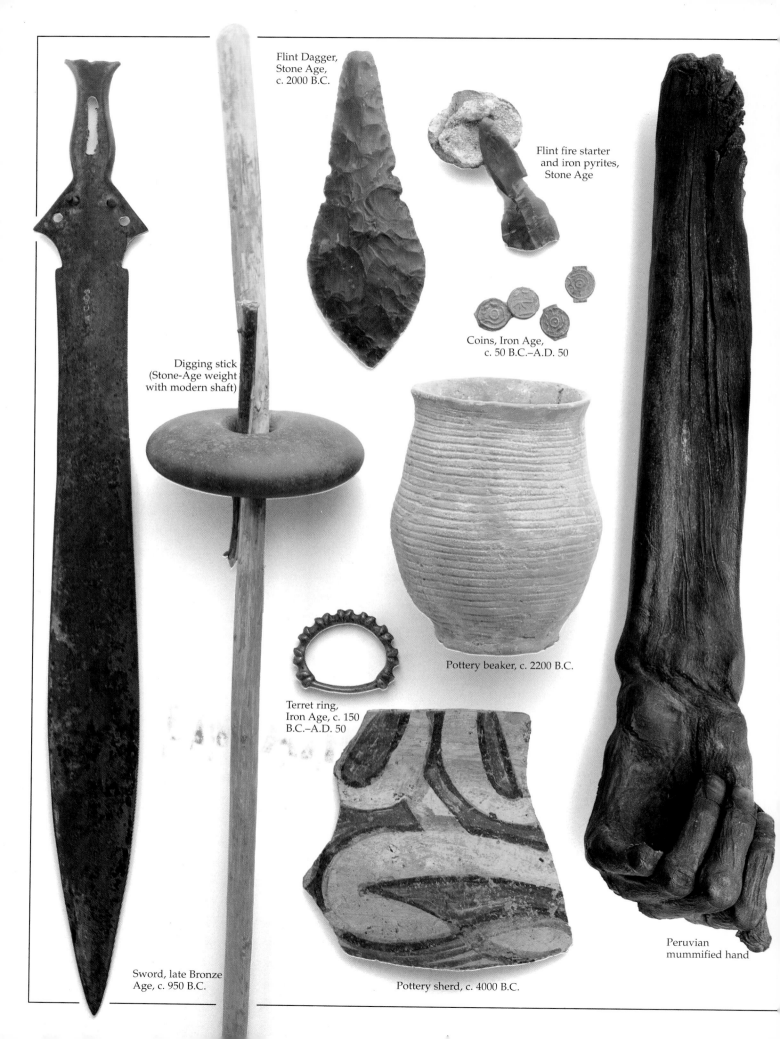

Flint Dagger,
Stone Age,
c. 2000 B.C.

Flint fire starter
and iron pyrites,
Stone Age

Coins, Iron Age,
c. 50 B.C.–A.D. 50

Digging stick
(Stone-Age weight
with modern shaft)

Pottery beaker, c. 2200 B.C.

Terret ring,
Iron Age, c. 150
B.C.–A.D. 50

Sword, late Bronze
Age, c. 950 B.C.

Pottery sherd, c. 4000 B.C.

Peruvian
mummified hand

Sage

Eyewitness
EARLY HUMANS

Almonds

Comb, Amazon rain forest

Fire and fire stones

Arrows, as
used c. 6000 B.C.

Flint handaxe, Stone Age,
c. 200,000 B.C.

DK

DK Publishing, Inc.

Antler harpoon point

Antler comb for preparing animal hides

Plumed comb,
Papua New Guinea

DK

LONDON, NEW YORK, MUNICH,
MELBOURNE, and DELHI

Project editor Phil Wilkinson
Art editor Miranda Kennedy
Managing editor Vicky Davenport
Managing art editor Jane Owen
Special photography Dave King
Editorial consultant Nick Merriman

REVISED EDITION
Managing editors Linda Esposito, Andrew Macintyre
Managing art editor Jane Thomas
Category publisher Linda Martin
Art director Simon Webb
Editor and reference compiler Clare Hibbert
Art editor Joanna Pocock
Consultant Ben Morgan
Production Jenny Jacoby
Picture research Celia Dearing
DTP designer Siu Yin Ho

U.S. editors Elizabeth Hester, John Searcy
Publishing director Beth Sutinis
Art director Dirk Kaufman
U.S. DTP designer Milos Orlovic
U.S. production Chris Avgherinos, Ivor Parker

This Eyewitness ® Guide has been conceived by
Dorling Kindersley Limited and Editions Gallimard

This edition published in the United States in 2005
by DK Publishing, Inc.
375 Hudson Street, New York, NY 10014

06 07 08 09 10 9 8 7 6 5 4 3 2

A catalog record for this book is
available from the Library of Congress.

ISBN-13: 978 0 7566 1067 8 (plc)
ISBN-13: 978 0 7566 1068 5 (alb)

Color reproduction by
Colourscan, Singapore
Printed in China by Toppan Co.,
(Shenzhen) Ltd.

Discover more at
www.dk.com

Soay sheep's wool
on spindle

Flint arrowheads,
c. 2000 B.C.

Iron-Age bronze
bracelet, c. 50 B.C.

Contents

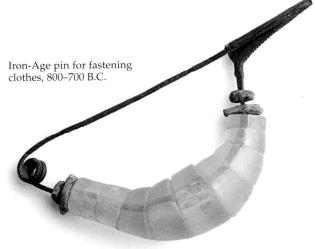

Iron-Age pin for fastening clothes, 800–700 B.C.

Human or ape?

IN AFRICA around ten million years ago, the climate was changing and grassland was replacing forest. To make use of this new environment, the early apes started to spend more time on the ground. They foraged for plants and scavenged animal remains, and this encouraged cooperation, communication, and increased intelligence. By around six million years ago, the ape family had split into two distinct branches, the one that led to chimpanzees, and the one that led to humans. Members of this human branch are usually known as the *Hominidae* or hominids; some experts prefer to call them hominins. Hominids are distinguished from their more apelike ancestors by their bigger brains, different teeth, and upright walking (which left their hands free for other tasks). One of the earliest known groups to exhibit these features are called australopithecines ("southern apes"), and were present from four to one million years ago.

The smallest species of australopithecine, shown here with a modern woman, was the size of an upright chimpanzee. Other species were as tall as we are.

OUT OF AFRICA
Australopithecines have been found only in E. and S. Africa. It is not clear whether humans first evolved in the area, or whether the fossils are just best preserved there.

EARLY BIRD
The lesser flamingo frequented shallow lakes in East Africa at the time of the earliest hominids.

ARMS AND HANDS
Lucy walked upright, so her hands were freer than those of apes. She did not make tools, but probably used convenient stones for some tasks.

FOOTPRINTS IN THE ASH
In 1976, the footprints of two australopithecines, an adult and a child walking side by side, were found on this site. They had walked over freshly laid volcanic ash, which had then hardened. A third australopithecine also seems to have walked in the adult's footprints.

IN THE GRASSLANDS
This is a reconstruction of a scene at Laetoli in East Africa about 3.75 million years ago. The region was covered by tropical grassland with lakes and a few shady trees. Early hominids foraged for food and walked upright so they could see over the tall grass.

"LUCY"
In 1974, the oldest and most complete australopithecine skeleton found so far was excavated (dug up) in Ethiopia (East Africa). It was named "Lucy," after the Beatles song "Lucy in the Sky with Diamonds," which was playing in the excavators' camp at the time

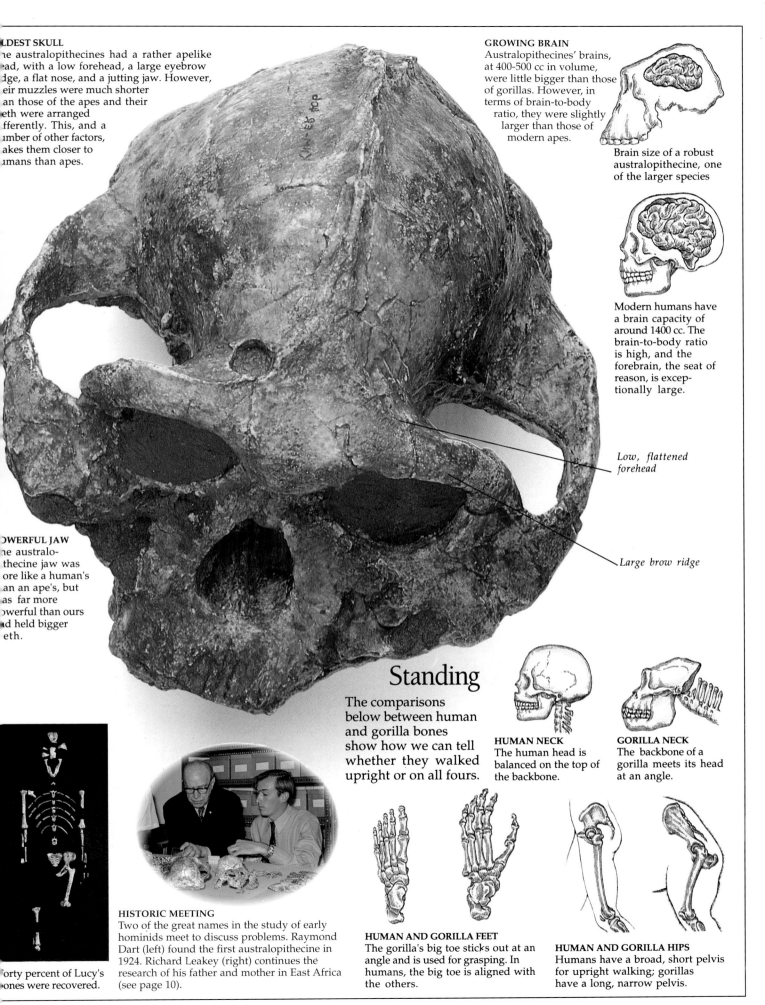

...LDEST SKULL
...he australopithecines had a rather apelike ...ad, with a low forehead, a large eyebrow ...dge, a flat nose, and a jutting jaw. However, ...eir muzzles were much shorter ...an those of the apes and their ...eth were arranged ...fferently. This, and a ...mber of other factors, ...akes them closer to ...umans than apes.

GROWING BRAIN
Australopithecines' brains, at 400-500 cc in volume, were little bigger than those of gorillas. However, in terms of brain-to-body ratio, they were slightly larger than those of modern apes.

Brain size of a robust australopithecine, one of the larger species

Modern humans have a brain capacity of around 1400 cc. The brain-to-body ratio is high, and the forebrain, the seat of reason, is exceptionally large.

Low, flattened forehead

...OWERFUL JAW
...he australo- ...thecine jaw was ...ore like a human's ...an an ape's, but ...as far more ...owerful than ours ...d held bigger ...eth.

Large brow ridge

Standing

The comparisons below between human and gorilla bones show how we can tell whether they walked upright or on all fours.

HUMAN NECK
The human head is balanced on the top of the backbone.

GORILLA NECK
The backbone of a gorilla meets its head at an angle.

HISTORIC MEETING
Two of the great names in the study of early hominids meet to discuss problems. Raymond Dart (left) found the first australopithecine in 1924. Richard Leakey (right) continues the research of his father and mother in East Africa (see page 10).

(see page 10)

...orty percent of Lucy's ...ones were recovered.

HUMAN AND GORILLA FEET
The gorilla's big toe sticks out at an angle and is used for grasping. In humans, the big toe is aligned with the others.

HUMAN AND GORILLA HIPS
Humans have a broad, short pelvis for upright walking; gorillas have a long, narrow pelvis.

Prehistoric food

Rue

Catmint

NETTLES
The young leaves of nettles were made into a soup. Nettle juice was used in cheese making.

ALTHOUGH WE DO NOT KNOW exactly what the earliest people ate, prehistoric people clearly had a very close relationship with the animals and plants around them. For thousands of years they lived as hunter-gatherers, living off the game that they hunted and the plants that they gathered. Through experience they learned what they could eat, and even which plants could treat illnesses. The prehistoric diet was surprisingly varied and included many plants we now think of as weeds. After people started to grow crops (see pages 30-31), nutritious wild foods were still eaten. These foods could only be preserved by drying, salting, or pickling, so the seasons had a strong effect on what was eaten. Another difference from our diet was that there were few sweeteners, except for honey.

MEDICINE
As well as being nutritious, many plants have medicinal properties that have been put to use for thousands of years. The leaves of rue were used for headaches; catmint was an ancient cold cure.

Wheat grains

Sunflower seeds

Dandelion leaves

An imaginative reconstruction of Stone Age hunter-gatherers preparing and cooking food

Juniper berries

SALAD DAYS
Although now thought of as weeds, dandelion leaves were a regular salad food in prehistoric times.

Hazelnuts

Almonds

FROM THE WOODS
Woodlands yielded an abundant supply of wild nuts and berries, which are excellent sources of nutrition and can easily be stored. Hazelnuts in particular seem to have been stored for the winter, and fruit could be preserved in the form of jam. In the Near East, wheat grains were first collected wild, and then cultivated. Juniper berries made a tasty spice.

Hazel twig

FOODS FOR THE FAMILY
As far as we know from recent societies, prehistoric hunter-gatherers benefited from a very broad diet, and each member of the family played his or her part in providing food. The men hunted wild animals, such as the stag shown here. The bulk of the food, however, was often gathered by the women and children. This consisted of such items as plants, eggs, nuts, and perhaps fish.

Quails' eggs

FRUIT
Fruit was an important food for early Mediterranean peoples. As well as being a rich source of nutrition, it could be dried and stored. Grapes could also be made into wine.

Figs

Dates

SALMON
From at least 10,000 B.C., people used large spears to catch salmon in the rivers of Europe.

Fenugreek

SPICE OF LIFE
Besides salt, which was used more to preserve food than to flavor it, a variety of seasonings and spices have a long history. Some, such as coriander, were also prized because they are good for the digestive system.

Coriander

Black cumin

Mustard

Peppercorns

HUNTING
This cave painting shows men hunting giant elk.

Seals were good food sources for northern peoples.

Basil

Mint

Sage

COOKING MEAT
This is a reconstruction of one ancient method of cooking meat. The meat was wrapped in a piece of leather and secured with a twig. This was put into a pot of water brought to boiling point by dropping in red-hot stones which had been heated in a fire (pp. 16-17). The more usual method of cooking meat was by putting it on a spit and grilling or roasting it over the glowing embers of a fire. Roasting was also done in a pit lined with heated stones.

HERBS
In prehistoric times, as now, herbs were often gathered to flavor food.

The toolmakers

ABOUT 2.4 MILLION YEARS AGO one of the australopithecine species gave rise to a new type of hominid, the genus *Homo*. Compared with *Australopithecus*, *Homo* had a bigger brain, a more human-looking face, and hip bones that were better adapted to walking upright and giving birth to babies with large heads. The earliest known species of the genus *Homo* could make tools and was therefore named *Homo habilis* ("handy man"). Toolmaking involves using memory, planning ahead, and working out abstract problems; it marks the beginning of our use of culture to help us adapt to our surroundings – a uniquely human ability. The early toolmakers probably also used some primitive form of communication to pass on knowledge. They seem to have used their tools to cut meat and smash open bones for marrow. They may possibly have hunted animals, but it is more likely that they scavenged abandoned carcasses, and that plants were still their major source of food. There is evidence that they also made small, round huts to shelter in – the earliest buildings in the world. They lived in East Africa, and related groups may have lived in South Africa and Southeast Asia.

PEBBLE TOOL
There is a great difference between using tools and manufacturing them. Chimpanzees may select certain items and change them for use as tools, but humans are the only animals to use one set of tools to make other tools. This pebble tool comes from Olduvai Gorge in Tanzania (East Africa).

The Piltdown forgery

Earlier this century, scientists were looking for a "missing link" between humans and apes. Between 1912 and 1915 amateur archaeologist Charles Dawson, and later Sir Arthur Smith Woodward of the British Museum, found a human skull with an ape's jaw in a gravel pit at Piltdown, England, together with bones of extinct animals. For years "Piltdown man" was accepted until 1953, when it was shown to be an elaborate forgery. Who carried out the hoax is still uncertain.

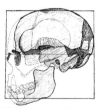

The Piltdown skull was made from an orangutan jaw stuck to a human skull

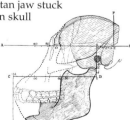

Orangutan skull

THE LEAKEY FAMILY
The Leakey family has been involved in research in East Africa for nearly sixty years. In 1960, years of patient work paid off for Louis Leakey and his wife Mary when they found and named the first *Homo habilis*. Their son, Richard, pictured here, has continued their work in Ethiopia, finding many more hominid remains.

This old drawing of an orangutan stresses its human-like characteristics.

Sir Arthur Smith Woodward of the British Museum.

PILTDOWN RECONSTRUCTION
So eager were scientists to find a missing link that many accepted the genuineness of Piltdown man immediately, and a number of reconstructions such as this one were soon made.

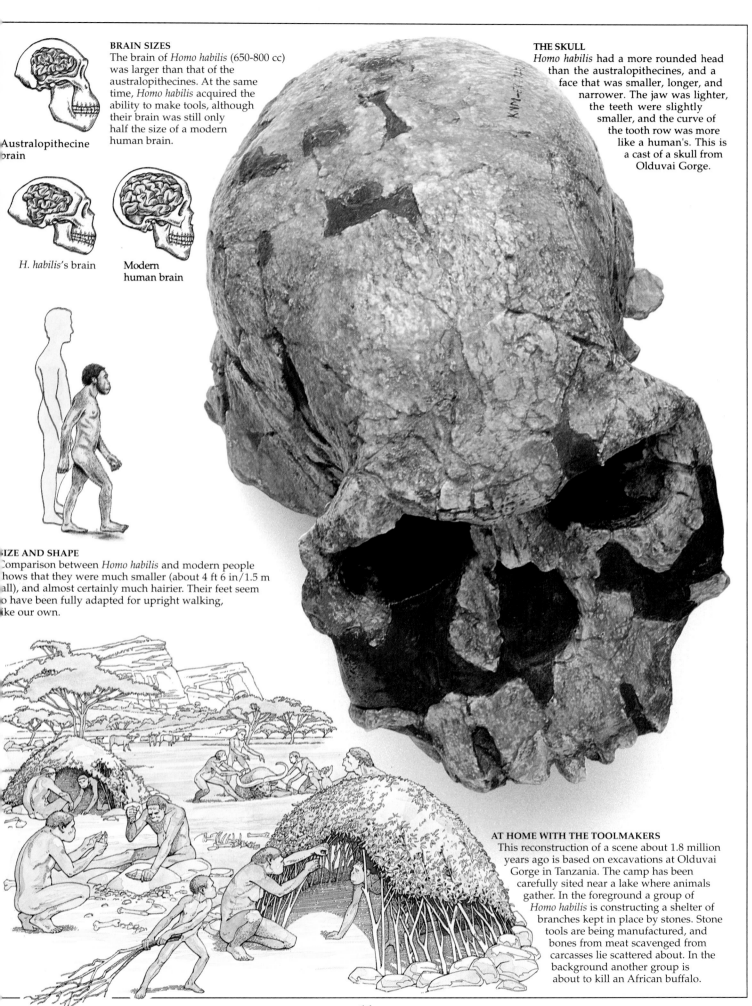

BRAIN SIZES
The brain of *Homo habilis* (650-800 cc) was larger than that of the australopithecines. At the same time, *Homo habilis* acquired the ability to make tools, although their brain was still only half the size of a modern human brain.

Australopithecine brain

H. habilis's brain

Modern human brain

THE SKULL
Homo habilis had a more rounded head than the australopithecines, and a face that was smaller, longer, and narrower. The jaw was lighter, the teeth were slightly smaller, and the curve of the tooth row was more like a human's. This is a cast of a skull from Olduvai Gorge.

SIZE AND SHAPE
Comparison between *Homo habilis* and modern people shows that they were much smaller (about 4 ft 6 in/1.5 m tall), and almost certainly much hairier. Their feet seem to have been fully adapted for upright walking, like our own.

AT HOME WITH THE TOOLMAKERS
This reconstruction of a scene about 1.8 million years ago is based on excavations at Olduvai Gorge in Tanzania. The camp has been carefully sited near a lake where animals gather. In the foreground a group of *Homo habilis* is constructing a shelter of branches kept in place by stones. Stone tools are being manufactured, and bones from meat scavenged from carcasses lie scattered about. In the background another group is about to kill an African buffalo.

Flintworking

THE FIRST TOOL-MAKING HUMAN, *Homo habilis*, made simple pebble tools from various types of rock (see pages 10-11). Later, in Europe, people found that flint was the most suitable material, and flint tools half a million years old have been found. Flint's most useful property is that regular flakes come off when it is chipped. The angle and size of the flakes can be controlled by careful chipping, and so a variety of sizes and shapes can be made. Because it is a little like glass, flint holds a very sharp edge that can be resharpened by further flaking when it is blunt. Flint is widespread and abundant, though in many cases it has to be mined from the chalk in which it occurs. The earliest tools were the flint flakes and cores used by *Homo habilis*. The flakes could be used to make finer tools and weapons, such as knives and arrowheads. Handaxes came later, with *Homo erectus* (see page 14-15).

FIRST IN ENGLAND
This handaxe is about a quarter of a million years old. It comes from Swanscombe, one of the oldest sites in England, where the earliest British human skull has been found.

Rounded end used as hammer head

Flat striking platform

CORE
A flint lump, or core, was often just the right shape for a simple tool.

Flint flake

Flint flake

HAMMERSTONE
A pebble hammer like this was the simplest tool used for flintworking. The unworked flint was struck with the hammer, and large, thick flakes came away.

2 REMOVING FLAKES
A stone hammer was used to strike a sharp blow along the edge of the rough-cut flint. This removed a large chip from the underside.

ANTLER HAMMER
A light bone or antler hammer was used for chipping off smaller, thinner pieces of flint.

1 SHAPING THE CORE
The first step in flintworking was to select a piece of flint and to start trimming it to a rough shape.

3 FINISHING
The axe was trimmed by striking it along its edge with a bone hammer.

FLINT FLAKE
Long, thin blades such as these are made by preparing a flat platform on a core and striking the outside rim vertically with a bone hammer.

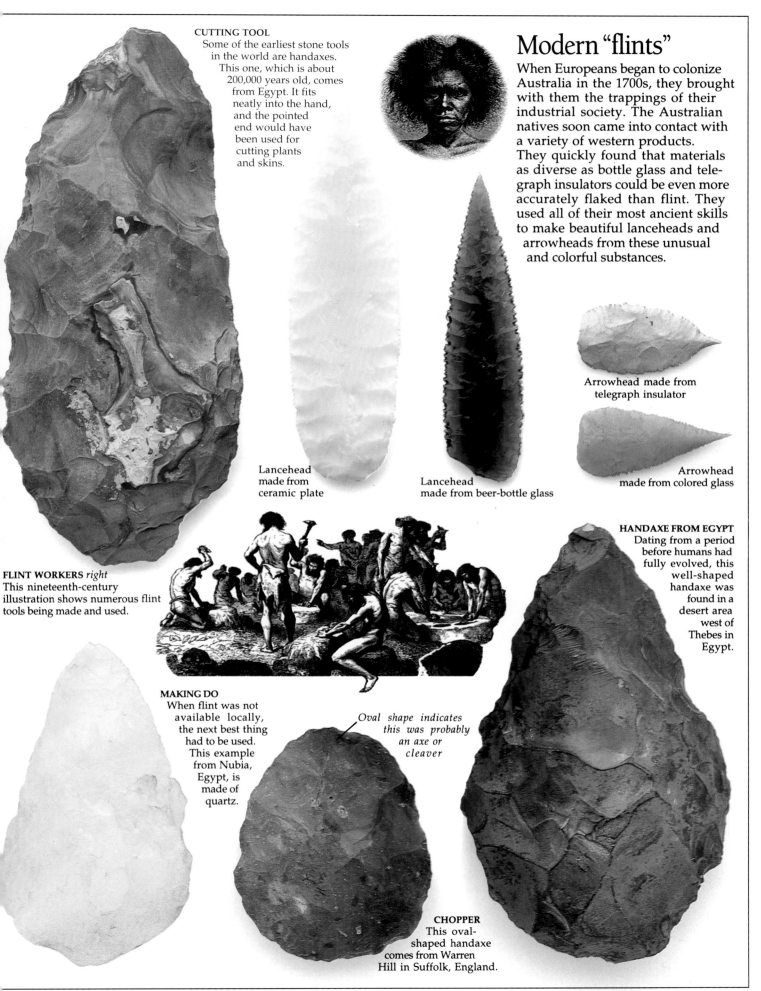

CUTTING TOOL
Some of the earliest stone tools in the world are handaxes. This one, which is about 200,000 years old, comes from Egypt. It fits neatly into the hand, and the pointed end would have been used for cutting plants and skins.

Modern "flints"

When Europeans began to colonize Australia in the 1700s, they brought with them the trappings of their industrial society. The Australian natives soon came into contact with a variety of western products. They quickly found that materials as diverse as bottle glass and telegraph insulators could be even more accurately flaked than flint. They used all of their most ancient skills to make beautiful lanceheads and arrowheads from these unusual and colorful substances.

Arrowhead made from telegraph insulator

Arrowhead made from colored glass

Lancehead made from ceramic plate

Lancehead made from beer-bottle glass

HANDAXE FROM EGYPT
Dating from a period before humans had fully evolved, this well-shaped handaxe was found in a desert area west of Thebes in Egypt.

FLINT WORKERS *right*
This nineteenth-century illustration shows numerous flint tools being made and used.

MAKING DO
When flint was not available locally, the next best thing had to be used. This example from Nubia, Egypt, is made of quartz.

Oval shape indicates this was probably an axe or cleaver

CHOPPER
This oval-shaped handaxe comes from Warren Hill in Suffolk, England.

Moving northwards

Between about 1.8 million and 200,000 years ago lived the species *Homo erectus*. They had bigger brains and bodies than *Homo habilis*, and some were probably as tall and as heavy as ourselves. They were also much more advanced than *Homo habilis* – they had more varied tools and may even have known how to use fire. Fire would have provided a focus for the family group, kept people warm, and been used for cooking. In addition, it could have been used for scaring predators or hunting game – animals could have been driven into traps using fire. With these skills, and the increased brain power that goes with them, *Homo erectus* ranged far beyond Africa into Europe and Asia, where most of their fossils have in fact been found. In these environments, the harshest of which would have been Ice Age Europe, *Homo erectus* gradually adapted to local conditions. Over a million years, they evolved differently in different parts of the world, but the fossils still share enough general characteristics to show clearly that they are ancestors of ours.

THE SPREAD OF *HOMO ERECTUS*
Although *Homo erectus* probably started life in Africa, remains have been found in places as far away as China and Java. They colonized these areas by making short outward migrations into new territory away from each generation's family base.

WOOLLY RHINOCEROS
Homo erectus survived until well into the Ice Age, when, in Europe, colder conditions came and went at intervals of several thousand years (pp. 18-19). Adapted to this climate, the woolly rhinoceros was one of the large mammals that *Homo erectus* may have hunted.

Stick held in hand

FIRE STICKS
The earliest hominids might have made occasional use of natural fires caused by lightning, but *Homo erectus* seems to have been the first to create fire deliberately. A simple wooden tool like this would have been used to make fire.

Groove to take stick

Wooden hearth

FIRE MAKERS
This scene shows a band of *Homo erectus* people in front of the cave they are using for shelter. On the right a male is starting to make a handaxe by removing flakes from a flint core with a hammerstone (p. 12). The female next to him is kindling a fire in a hearth surrounded by stones to shelter it from the wind. The people in the background are using handaxes to butcher a large mammal they have hunted. The meat will then be cooked over the open fire.

A MORE HUMAN HEAD

The skull of *Homo erectus* has several features that make it look more human than that of *Homo habilis*. The brain is larger, ranging from 750 to 1250 cc in volume (compared with an average of 1,400 cc for modern humans). The teeth are smaller than those of *Homo habilis*. But the skull of *Homo erectus* is still different from a modern skull in many ways. It is very thick, with a sloping forehead and a large eyebrow ridge; there is a relatively massive jaw, flat face, and no chin; and the large jaw and teeth needed strong muscles to keep the head upright – these were attached to a bony bump at the back of the head.

Paleontologists have pieced together the fragments of skull, like a puzzle

Long, low skull

Sloping forehead

Strong eyebrow ridge

Lower jaw (not shown) joins skull here

Teeth smaller than those of Homo habilis, *but bigger than modern human's*

A NEW TYPE OF TOOL

The handaxe was the distinctive new type of tool produced by *Homo erectus*. The broad end was held in the fist, and the axe was used for cutting meat or digging up edible roots. Handaxes spread over the Old World and remained in use for about one and a half million years.

EVIDENCE FOR FIRE

Charred remains found in East Africa hint that *Homo erectus* may have had fire as long as 1.4 million years ago, but scientists are not sure about this. Some of the best evidence that *H. erectus* had fire comes from a cave called Zhoukoudian near Beijing, China. Inside, many *H. erectus* remains were found, dating back 360,000 years. A deep layer of ash suggested prolonged use of fire, as did large lumps of charcoal (right) and burned bone from animals that had been killed and eaten (above).

The coming of fire

FIRE WAS ONE OF THE MOST IMPORTANT DISCOVERIES ever made by ancient people. It not only enabled them to keep warm when the temperature was very much colder than it is today, but was also useful in keeping wild animals away, roasting meat, and hardening the tips of wooden spears. Prehistoric people also sometimes deliberately set fire to forests to clear the ground, making hunting and agriculture easier. Before they learned to make fire, people probably used accidental fires caused by lightning. The great step forward was made when they found out how to make fire for themselves, perhaps by rubbing two sticks together extremely quickly to create a spark. Experts are not sure when humans first discovered how to start fires, but evidence from France and China suggests that *Homo erectus* was using fire about 400,000 years ago. Because fires were so difficult to start, people tried to keep them burning continuously, rather than relighting them.

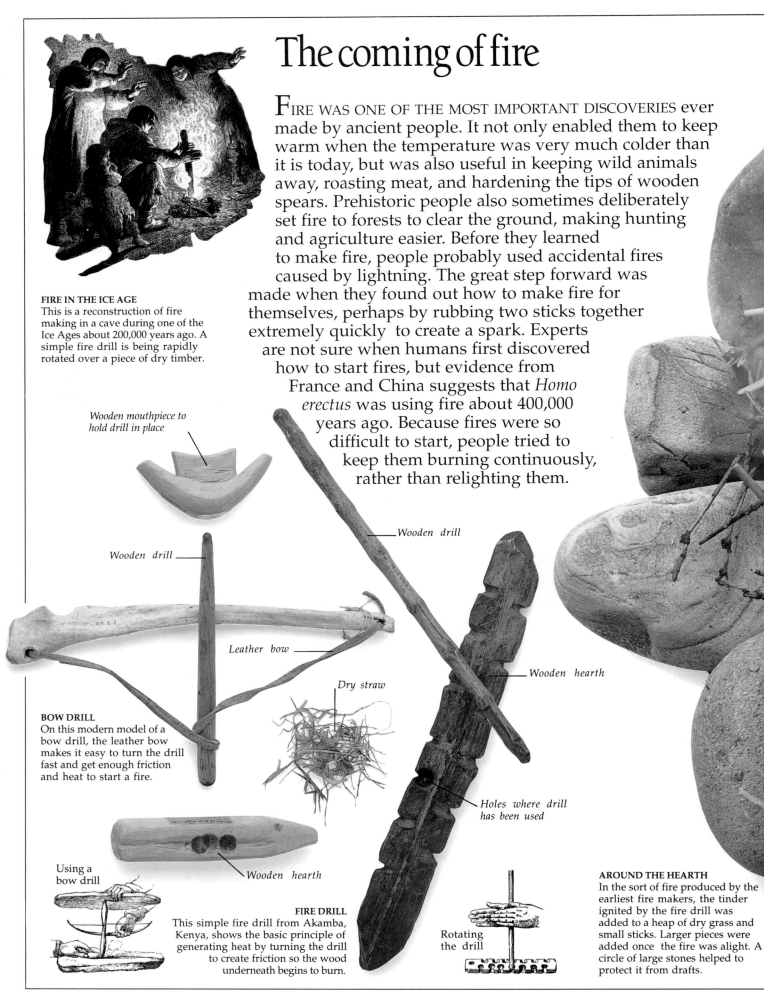

FIRE IN THE ICE AGE
This is a reconstruction of fire making in a cave during one of the Ice Ages about 200,000 years ago. A simple fire drill is being rapidly rotated over a piece of dry timber.

Wooden mouthpiece to hold drill in place

Wooden drill

Wooden drill

Leather bow

Dry straw

Wooden hearth

Holes where drill has been used

BOW DRILL
On this modern model of a bow drill, the leather bow makes it easy to turn the drill fast and get enough friction and heat to start a fire.

Using a bow drill

Wooden hearth

FIRE DRILL
This simple fire drill from Akamba, Kenya, shows the basic principle of generating heat by turning the drill to create friction so the wood underneath begins to burn.

Rotating the drill

AROUND THE HEARTH
In the sort of fire produced by the earliest fire makers, the tinder ignited by the fire drill was added to a heap of dry grass and small sticks. Larger pieces were added once the fire was alight. A circle of large stones helped to protect it from drafts.

TWO DRY STICKS?
In the Stone Age, people started fires using brushwood and the spark produced when they struck flint against a mineral called iron pyrite (fool's gold). Perhaps they found this out by accident while making stone tools. This method would have been far easier than rubbing together dry sticks, as shown here.

Sticks would be built up as the fire started to burn

As the stones got hot they could be used to heat water for cooking

AFRICAN FIRE MAKING
Much of our knowledge of early fire-making techniques comes from studies of early African tools such as the simple wooden drill.

Life in the Ice Age

THE "ICE AGE" consisted of several alternate cold and warm periods, each lasting tens of thousands of years. During some of these periods the climate was actually warmer than it is today, and only for parts of the period was there extensive ice coverage of northern Europe. The *Homo erectus* people were the first to live in this area, probably only in the warm periods. By 250,000 years ago, people were slowly adapting to living in the cold periods, and by 120,000 years ago, a distinct human species – *Homo neanderthalensis* – can be recognized. Although close cousins of modern humans, Neanderthals looked very different. They had short, stocky bodies and were very muscular – even the children. They had large heads, huge projecting noses, and deep-set eyes under a prominent brow ridge. Neanderthals show the first stirrings of humanity: they cared for the disabled, buried their dead carefully, and probably had some sort of religion. They were abruptly replaced about 35,000 years ago by fully modern people, *Homo sapiens*, who had been evolving in the meantime in the warmer climate of Africa. They colonized huge areas of the world at this time, including Europe in its final icy phase, and even Australia.

THE ICE AGE AND THE NEANDERTHALS
This map shows the maximum extent of the ice sheets (blue), and the land exposed by the consequent lowering of the sea level. The spread of Neanderthals over a period of 60,000 years is indicated in brown, and the red dot shows the Neander Valley in Germany, where the first find was made in 1856.

HOME ON THE TUNDRA
When *Homo sapiens* colonized the cold Russian tundra, they built tents – a method that may also have been employed by the Neanderthals, in places where there were few caves. This reconstruction shows a dwelling excavated at Pushkari, consisting of sewn skins stretched over a frame of poles, weighted down by mammoth bones.

TOOLMAKING
Neanderthal tools were a great improvement on those used by *Homo erectus*. They could produce a wide range of fine, stone tools for a variety of tasks. They may have used bone and antler, as well as flint.

LIFE IN A COLD CLIMATE
Neanderthals were well adapted for living in a cold climate, and their lifestyle may in some respects have resembled that of today's Inuit people (see pages 20-21). They probably lived in extended family groups, with each member responsible for a variety of tasks. It is even possible that they may have developed a restricted range of speech (see page 65).

CAVE CULTURE
The Neanderthals lived in caves that had cozy hearths. They had advanced stone tools for hunting and preparing food. They buried their dead, and they also made simple ornaments, such as pendants with holes for string, probably made from a length of animal sinew.

THE NEANDERTHAL WARDROBE
Neanderthals were probably the first humans to wear clothes much of the time, to protect themselves from the cold. When making clothes, they would begin by stretching out an animal hide such as a deerskin, and use flint tools to scrape it clean of fat and sinew. After tanning, they would sew the hide into the required shape.

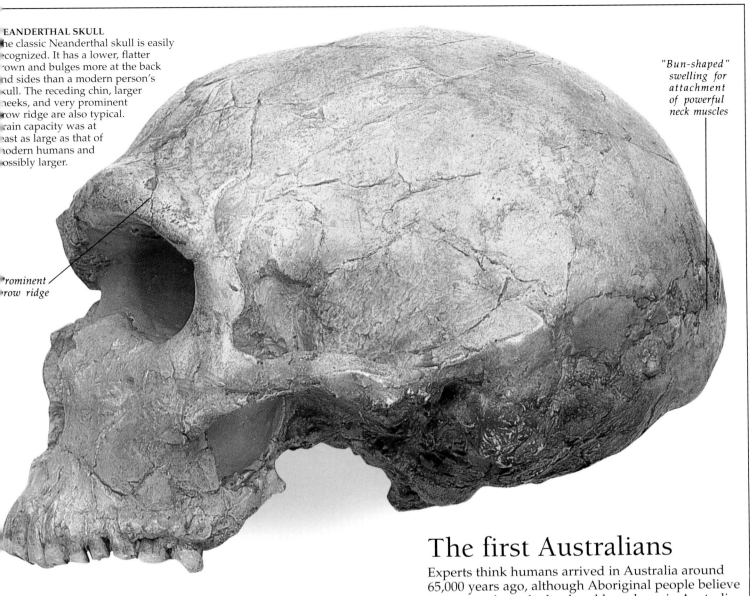

NEANDERTHAL SKULL

The classic Neanderthal skull is easily recognized. It has a lower, flatter crown and bulges more at the back and sides than a modern person's skull. The receding chin, larger cheeks, and very prominent brow ridge are also typical. Brain capacity was at least as large as that of modern humans and possibly larger.

Prominent brow ridge

"Bun-shaped" swelling for attachment of powerful neck muscles

SCRAPER

By the time of the Neanderthals, people were able to make a wide variety of stone tools and weapons, using flakes struck from a prepared core (p. 12). This is a flint scraper for preparing skins.

The first Australians

Experts think humans arrived in Australia around 65,000 years ago, although Aboriginal people believe they came from the land and have been in Australia forever. The earliest human remains found are those of fully modern people, *Homo sapiens*, who may have come from the islands of Southeast Asia. Some later skulls show older traits, so a mixture of groups may have colonized the area.

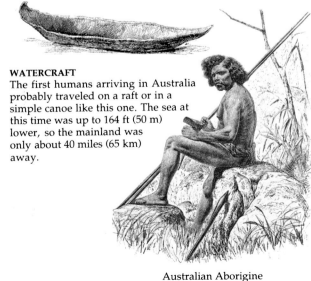

WATERCRAFT

The first humans arriving in Australia probably traveled on a raft or in a simple canoe like this one. The sea at this time was up to 164 ft (50 m) lower, so the mainland was only about 40 miles (65 km) away.

THE NEANDERTHALS' IMAGE

Neanderthals have long been portrayed as primitive savages, as in the artwork above. However, despite their formidable appearance, they were sophisticated people who used fire, made clothes, and managed to survive in the freezing climate of Ice Age Europe.

Australian Aborigine

Ice Age hunters

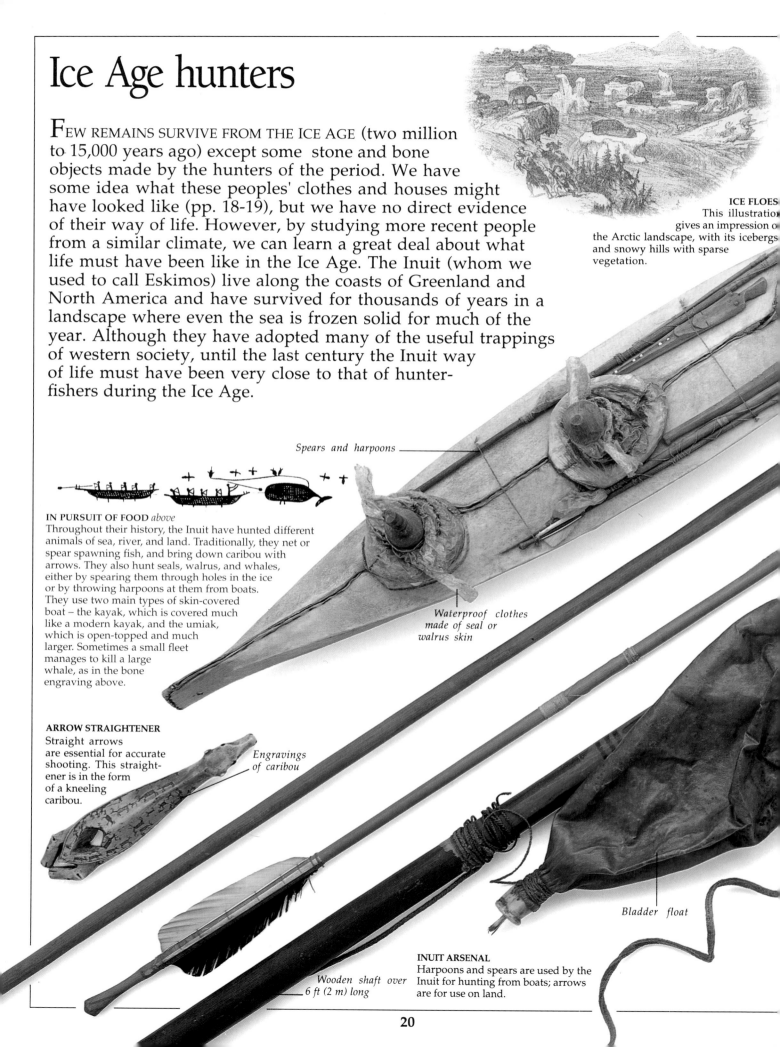

FEW REMAINS SURVIVE FROM THE ICE AGE (two million to 15,000 years ago) except some stone and bone objects made by the hunters of the period. We have some idea what these peoples' clothes and houses might have looked like (pp. 18-19), but we have no direct evidence of their way of life. However, by studying more recent people from a similar climate, we can learn a great deal about what life must have been like in the Ice Age. The Inuit (whom we used to call Eskimos) live along the coasts of Greenland and North America and have survived for thousands of years in a landscape where even the sea is frozen solid for much of the year. Although they have adopted many of the useful trappings of western society, until the last century the Inuit way of life must have been very close to that of hunter-fishers during the Ice Age.

ICE FLOES
This illustration gives an impression of the Arctic landscape, with its icebergs and snowy hills with sparse vegetation.

Spears and harpoons

IN PURSUIT OF FOOD *above*
Throughout their history, the Inuit have hunted different animals of sea, river, and land. Traditionally, they net or spear spawning fish, and bring down caribou with arrows. They also hunt seals, walrus, and whales, either by spearing them through holes in the ice or by throwing harpoons at them from boats. They use two main types of skin-covered boat – the kayak, which is covered much like a modern kayak, and the umiak, which is open-topped and much larger. Sometimes a small fleet manages to kill a large whale, as in the bone engraving above.

Waterproof clothes made of seal or walrus skin

ARROW STRAIGHTENER
Straight arrows are essential for accurate shooting. This straightener is in the form of a kneeling caribou.

Engravings of caribou

Bladder float

Wooden shaft over 6 ft (2 m) long

INUIT ARSENAL
Harpoons and spears are used by the Inuit for hunting from boats; arrows are for use on land.

AYAK
This model of an Inuit kayak is fully equipped with miniature spears and harpoons. Waterproof coverings surround each figure and are secured with a drawstring to keep water from getting into the kayak.

Skin exterior

Protective skin covering

POWERFUL POINTS
When this harpoon is thrown, the ivory barbs dig into the animal. The hunter can tug the string at the rear of the weapon so the wounded animal cannot swim away.

LONG-DISTANCE WEAPON
A spear has no cord for pulling back. After firing, the hunter must run to the injured animal.

Ivory harpoon head

LYING IN WAIT
When the sea is frozen, the Inuit hunt seals through the ice. The seals have to come to holes in the ice in order to breathe, so the hunters wait until a seal appears at the surface.

WHALER'S WEAPON
Large harpoons such as this are hurled from boats at walruses or even whales. The bladder keeps the harpoon afloat if it misses the target, so that the hunter can retrieve it.

SNOW KNIVES
These two knives were made for cutting blocks of snow for igloo making. They are richly engraved with different scenes showing animals, hunters, and houses.

Thin viewing slits to eliminate glare

GOGGLES
These protect the wearer from the glare of the snow.

Skin line

BONE KNIVES
The Inuit are careful not to waste any part of the animals they hunt. Bone is used for tools and weapons. The one on the left has animal gut twined around the handle to give a better grip.

Hunting scene

CARVING
The Inuit have a strong tradition of carving. Here a craftsman is engraving a piece of ivory with a knife.

Modern humans

MOST EXPERTS BELIEVE that the species to which we belong, *Homo sapiens*, evolved in Africa, some time between 200,000 and 100,000 years ago. By 30,000 years ago, *H. sapiens* had spread to all parts of the world apart from the Americas; by at least 11,000 years ago, every continent apart from Antarctica was populated. *Homo sapiens* had more tools than their predecessors, including a wide variety of stone blades and tools made of bone, wood, and ivory. They lived in larger settlements, and there was more contact between villages and tribes. Communication through the spoken word and through art, engravings, sculpture, and music became a vital part of human life. Later human developments (farming, civilization, huge population growth, industry, and control over nature) have occurred in the relatively short period of 10,000 years.

PAINTED HAND
About 20,000 years ago in a cave at Pech-Merle in France, someone produced this "negative" hand by placing his or her hand on the wall and painting over it. The hand, the part of us that makes and uses tools and is used for signaling, is a powerful symbol.

"Venus" figurine in stone from Willendorf, Austria

WORKS OF ART
Although the Neanderthals were the first to show some artistic sense by scratching simple designs on bones, it was not until the arrival of *Homo sapiens* that painting and sculpture developed fully.

Stylized female figure from Corsica, c. 3500 B.C.

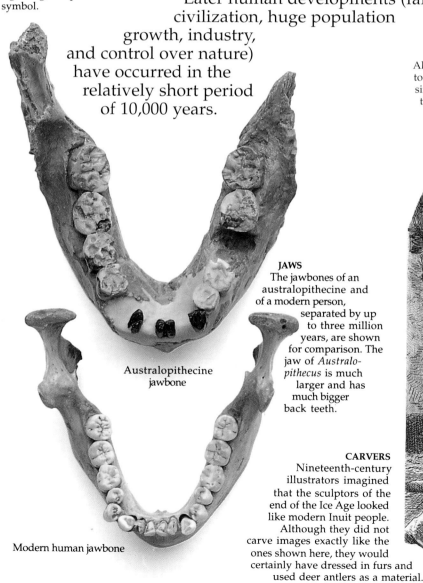

JAWS
The jawbones of an australopithecine and of a modern person, separated by up to three million years, are shown for comparison. The jaw of *Australopithecus* is much larger and has much bigger back teeth.

Australopithecine jawbone

Modern human jawbone

CARVERS
Nineteenth-century illustrators imagined that the sculptors of the end of the Ice Age looked like modern Inuit people. Although they did not carve images exactly like the ones shown here, they would certainly have dressed in furs and used deer antlers as a material.

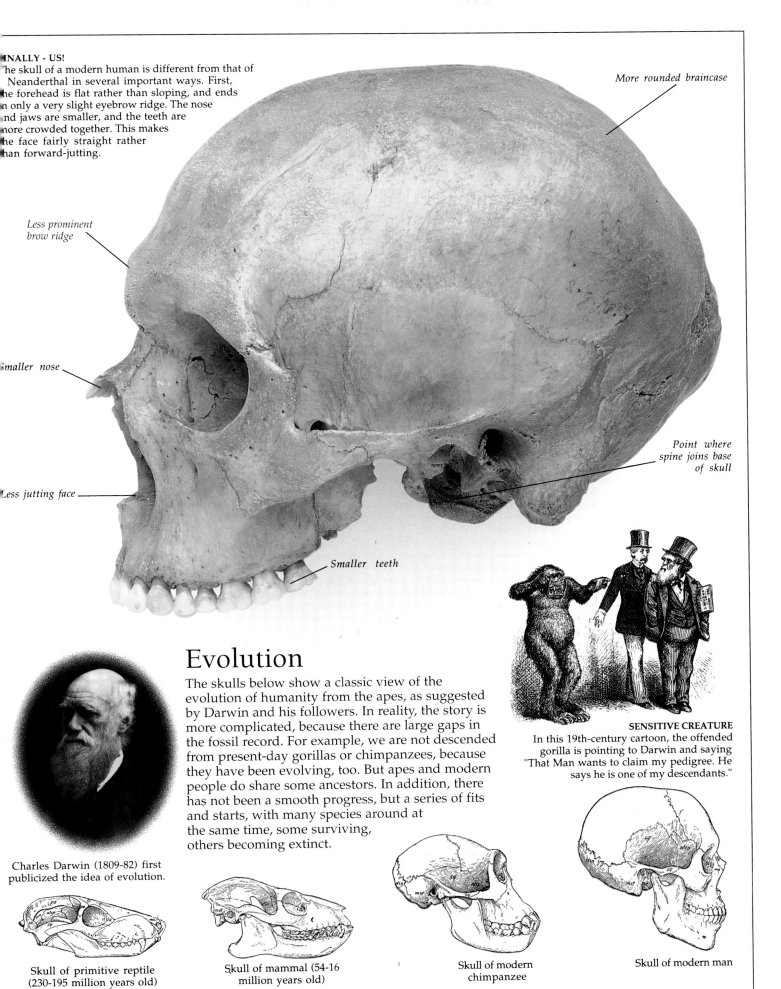

FINALLY - US!
The skull of a modern human is different from that of Neanderthal in several important ways. First, the forehead is flat rather than sloping, and ends in only a very slight eyebrow ridge. The nose and jaws are smaller, and the teeth are more crowded together. This makes the face fairly straight rather than forward-jutting.

More rounded braincase

Less prominent brow ridge

Smaller nose

Less jutting face

Point where spine joins base of skull

Smaller teeth

Evolution

The skulls below show a classic view of the evolution of humanity from the apes, as suggested by Darwin and his followers. In reality, the story is more complicated, because there are large gaps in the fossil record. For example, we are not descended from present-day gorillas or chimpanzees, because they have been evolving, too. But apes and modern people do share some ancestors. In addition, there has not been a smooth progress, but a series of fits and starts, with many species around at the same time, some surviving, others becoming extinct.

SENSITIVE CREATURE
In this 19th-century cartoon, the offended gorilla is pointing to Darwin and saying "That Man wants to claim my pedigree. He says he is one of my descendants."

Charles Darwin (1809-82) first publicized the idea of evolution.

Skull of primitive reptile (230-195 million years old)

Skull of mammal (54-16 million years old)

Skull of modern chimpanzee

Skull of modern man

The first artists

SOME OF THE EARLIEST WORKS OF ART were created around 30,000 years ago, during the last Ice Age. Because the making of art is peculiar to humankind, we can say with confidence that by this period the creators of such works were truly human. These early works of art take two main forms. The most famous are the vivid paintings of animals that cover the walls and roofs of caves, such as those at Lascaux in France and Altamira in Spain. The other, less well-known, type consists of small sculptures and relief carvings of animals and female figures. These have also been found in caves, but they occur in large numbers in open-air sites in eastern Europe. Decoration became popular again when pottery was invented.

MASTERPIECE OF CAVE ART
This painting is in a cave at Altamira, Spain.

From the ca̶ of Mas d'Azil, Fran̶

HORSES' HEAD̶
The accuracy of thes̶ carvings shows that th̶ artist must have observe̶ wild horses at close quarters̶

MAMMOTH CARVING
A skillful sculptor carved this animal's shoulder blade into a stylized mammoth with large tusks that curve around its head. Mammoths were common until the end of the Ice Age.

IN HOT PURSUIT *right*
The earliest artists carved pictures of the wild animals they hunted for food. This one is engraved on bone and shows a bison being followed by a human figure. It is from Laugerie Basse, France.

HUNTER'S QUARRY
A stag and four chamois are carved on this piece of bone. Similar to goat̶ chamois are still foun̶ in Europe.

GOOD-LUCK CHARM
This old illustration shows a man carving a piece of antler to bring success in hunting.

HORSE'S HEAD
This engraving on bone was found in a cave at Laugerie Basse, France.

MAKING THE COLORS *right*
In this reconstruction, an artist is grinding up a pigment to make paint. Early artists used earth colors such as ochres, and pigments made from other naturally occurring minerals.

PATTERNED PLAQUE
This plaque, made from a type of stone called schist, was produced over 4,000 years after cave painting had died out, and is engraved in a quite different, abstract, geometric style. It was found in a large stone tomb at Alentjo, Portugal, and dates from the New Stone Age (c. 4000 B.C.).

ARTISTS AT WORK
This artist is painting the animals he is going to hunt. This activity would have formed part of his religious ritual. Light for the painters was provided by burning fat in a lamp.

Marble figurine from Melos, Greece, c. 2500-2000 B.C.

PAINTED POTTERY
As well as being useful, pottery can also be strikingly painted and engraved. This example is about 6,000 years old and comes from Rumania.

BISON
This is another painting from the famous Spanish cave at Altamira.

Found at the site of Lespugue, France

THE POTTER'S ART
The decoration on many early pots was engraved in the surface of the clay.

MYSTERIOUS FIGURES
These so-called "Venus figurines" have been found across Europe, from Spain to Russia, and date from around 25,000 to 15,000 BC. They are always faceless and heavily pregnant. They seem to show the importance placed on reproduction and fertility.

From Brno, Czechoslovakia

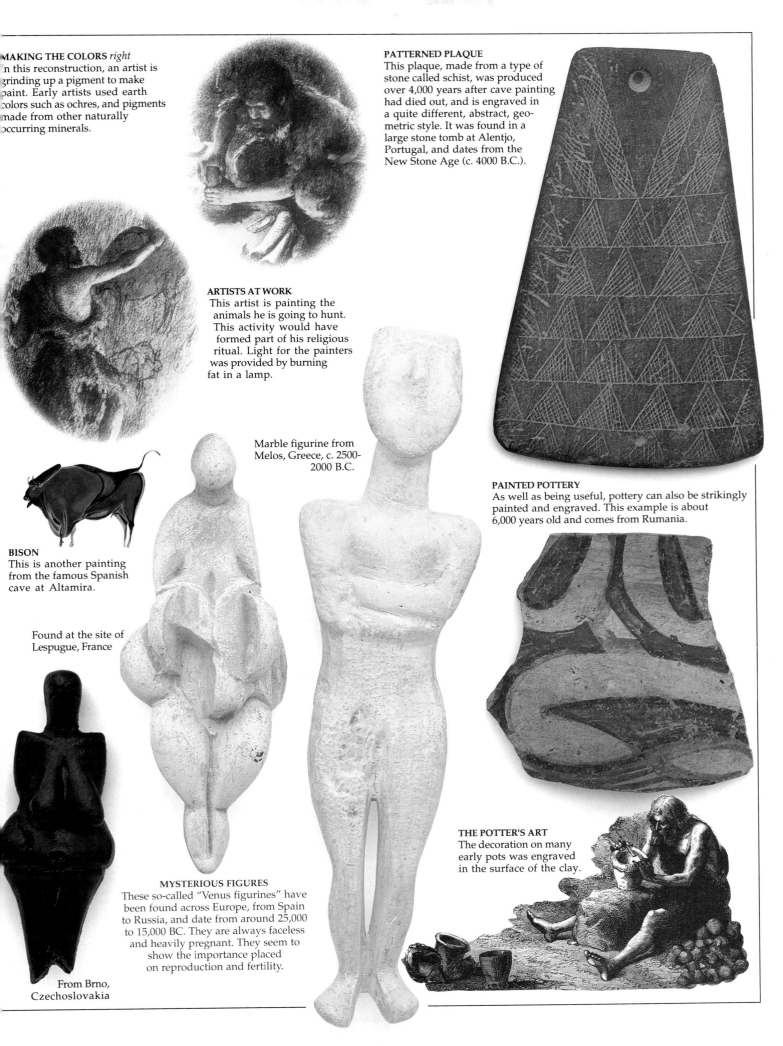

Hunting and gathering

STONE AGE HUNTERS
Both spears and bows and arrows were used to hunt for food in the Stone Age.

F OR NINETY-FIVE PER CENT of their time on earth, humans have survived by hunting animals and gathering plants for food. During the Ice Age, people in Europe were probably hunting big game such as the woolly mammoth. About 75,000 years ago, people on the coast of South Africa were catching seals and penguins; and 40,000 years ago the first Australians may have been hunting now-extinct giant kangaroos. Throughout the prehistoric period, it is likely that most of the hunter-gatherers' food came from plants, nuts, fruits, and shellfish, because these could be gathered with little effort. Their remains do not survive as well as bones, however, so they are not often found on archaeological sites. But the discovery of flint spear- and arrowheads suggests that early peoples had also evolved sophisticated hunting methods.

Bark "plate"

Blackberries

FRUIT AND NUTS
Remains of these high-energy foods have been found preserved in hunters' camps from 12,000 years ago.

Hazelnuts

HARPOON POINT
This point is made of antler and is about 10,000 years old.

Antler is easily made into harpoons like these

FISHING TACKLE *above*
Found near London, this harpoon would have been used for spearing fish from a sandbank at the river's edge. It dates from c. 8000 B.C.

Twine binding

SIMPLE BUT DEADLY *above and below*
Two halves of a reproduction of a middle Stone Age arrow. The bow and arrow were developed to hunt the shy forest animals from a distance.

Flight of duck feathers

Fire-hardened wooden point

Reproduction wooden shaft

FLINT ARROW
Arrows like this were used about 8,000 years ago. The head was stuck in place with birch resin glue.

Flints glued in groove cut in shaft

Reproduction shaft

Antler sleeve

Alternative method of binding

Wedge to prevent movement

DUAL-PURPOSE TOOL
This adze head is fitted into an antler sleeve and secured to the handle by a leather thong. It may have been used for digging up edible roots or for woodworking.

Wooden sleeve

Head dates from c. 10,000-4000 B.C.

Perforated quartzite pebble

FINEST FLINTS
In the early Bronze Age, a variety of finely worked flint arrowheads were produced. Some were shaped ornately.

Reproduction wooden handles

Traditional shape

SMALL FLINT ADZE
An adze has an uneven cutting edge and is mounted with the blade at right-angles to the handle. Used to cut wood, it is usually swung down, often between the legs. This one is inserted into a wooden sleeve and secured with animal glue or resin.

HUNTER'S PREY
Cave paintings, some 20,000 years old, often show animals that were hunted at the time, like this deer in the Dordogne, France.

Iron pyrite

Flint fire starter

Missing shaft

FIRE-MAKING
If the iron pyrite (fool's gold) is hit with a flint, a spark is produced. This will fall on dry grass and can be fanned into a flame.

Incurved design

This reindeer is being butchered with a stone axe.

Modern wooden stick

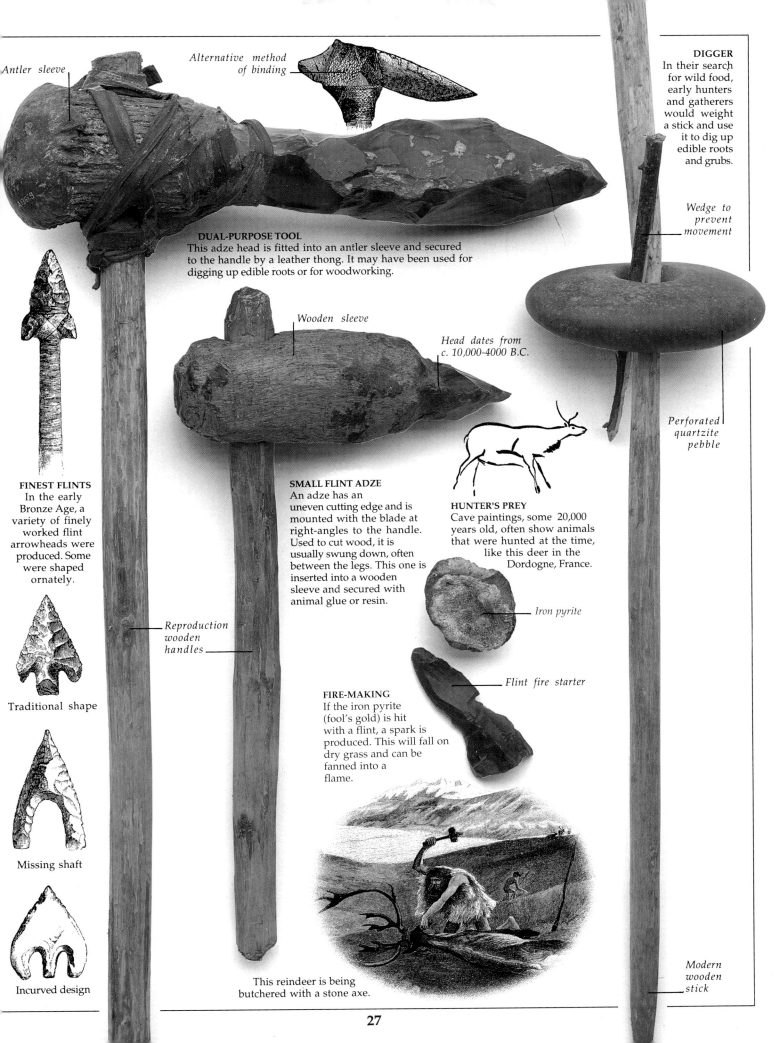

Hunters of the desert

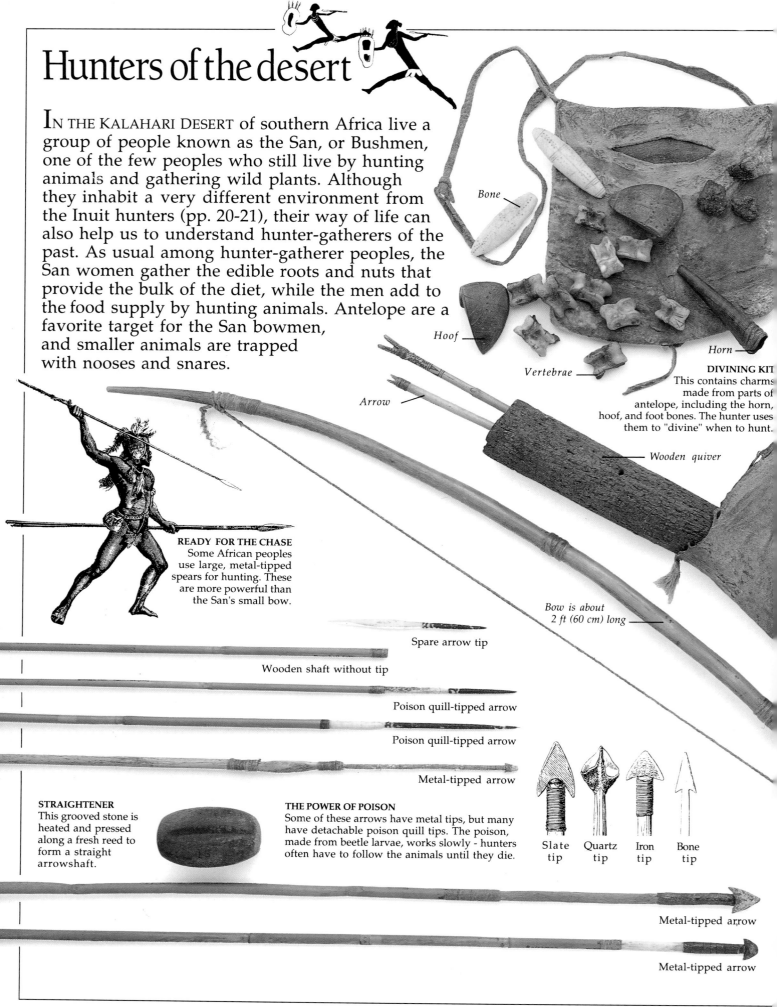

In the Kalahari Desert of southern Africa live a group of people known as the San, or Bushmen, one of the few peoples who still live by hunting animals and gathering wild plants. Although they inhabit a very different environment from the Inuit hunters (pp. 20-21), their way of life can also help us to understand hunter-gatherers of the past. As usual among hunter-gatherer peoples, the San women gather the edible roots and nuts that provide the bulk of the diet, while the men add to the food supply by hunting animals. Antelope are a favorite target for the San bowmen, and smaller animals are trapped with nooses and snares.

Bone

Hoof

Vertebrae

Arrow

Horn

DIVINING KIT
This contains charms made from parts of antelope, including the horn, hoof, and foot bones. The hunter uses them to "divine" when to hunt.

Wooden quiver

READY FOR THE CHASE
Some African peoples use large, metal-tipped spears for hunting. These are more powerful than the San's small bow.

Bow is about
2 ft (60 cm) long

Spare arrow tip

Wooden shaft without tip

Poison quill-tipped arrow

Poison quill-tipped arrow

Metal-tipped arrow

STRAIGHTENER
This grooved stone is heated and pressed along a fresh reed to form a straight arrowshaft.

THE POWER OF POISON
Some of these arrows have metal tips, but many have detachable poison quill tips. The poison, made from beetle larvae, works slowly - hunters often have to follow the animals until they die.

Slate tip

Quartz tip

Iron tip

Bone tip

Metal-tipped arrow

Metal-tipped arrow

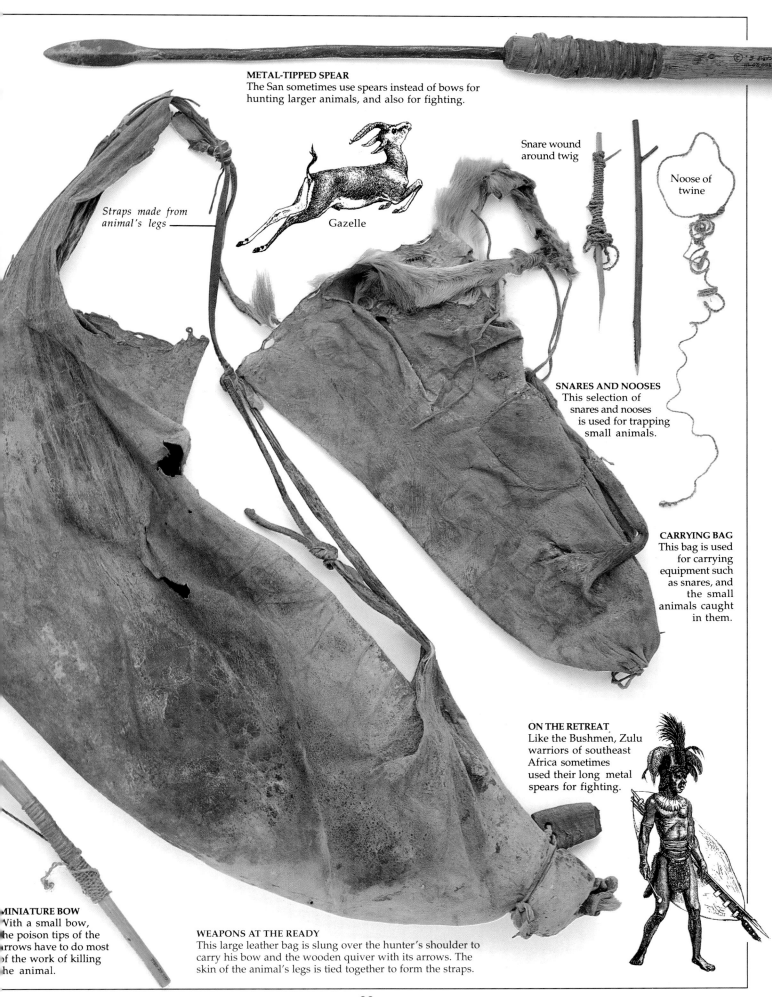

METAL-TIPPED SPEAR
The San sometimes use spears instead of bows for hunting larger animals, and also for fighting.

Gazelle

Snare wound around twig

Noose of twine

Straps made from animal's legs

SNARES AND NOOSES
This selection of snares and nooses is used for trapping small animals.

CARRYING BAG
This bag is used for carrying equipment such as snares, and the small animals caught in them.

ON THE RETREAT
Like the Bushmen, Zulu warriors of southeast Africa sometimes used their long metal spears for fighting.

MINIATURE BOW
With a small bow, the poison tips of the arrows have to do most of the work of killing the animal.

WEAPONS AT THE READY
This large leather bag is slung over the hunter's shoulder to carry his bow and the wooden quiver with its arrows. The skin of the animal's legs is tied together to form the straps.

Tilling the soil

HUMANITY'S GREATEST-EVER ADVANCEMENT, farming first began in the Near East around 10,000 B.C. and spread throughout Europe during the next six thousand years. It also developed independently in America, the Far East, and other areas of the world. The ability to grow plants and raise animals meant that people could control their sources of food rather than rely only on hunting and gathering. Farming enabled people to stay in one place all year round and to fill a greater number of mouths. As a result the population increased and towns began to develop.

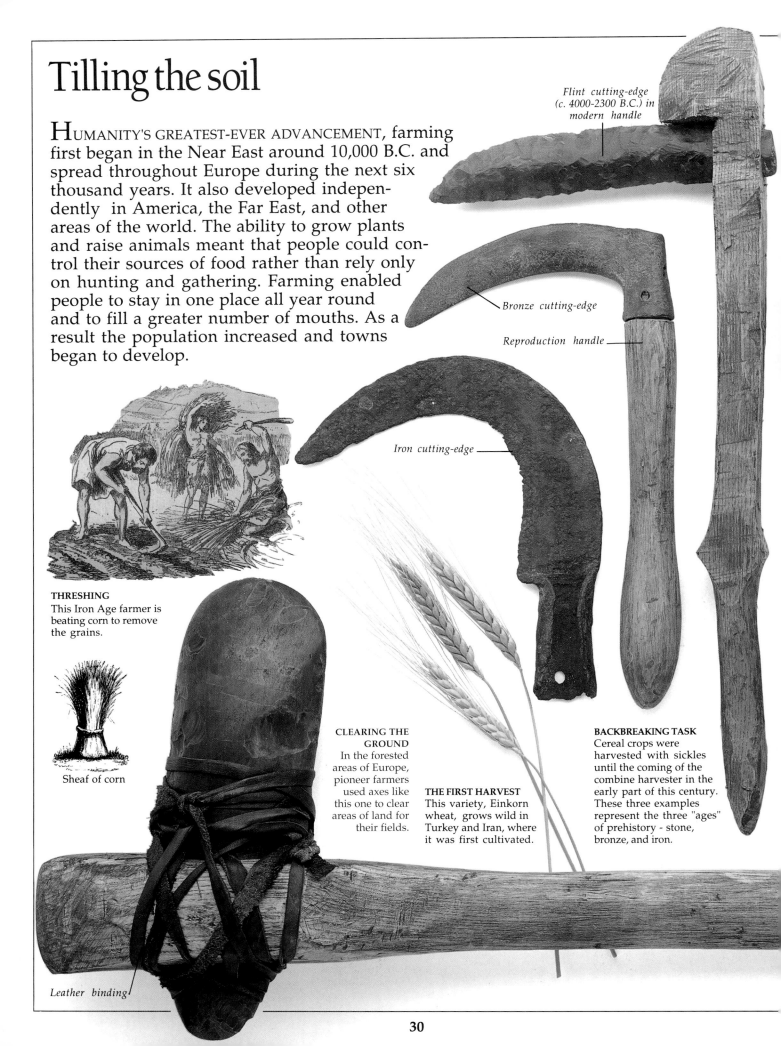

Flint cutting-edge (c. 4000-2300 B.C.) in modern handle

Bronze cutting-edge

Reproduction handle

Iron cutting-edge

THRESHING
This Iron Age farmer is beating corn to remove the grains.

Sheaf of corn

CLEARING THE GROUND
In the forested areas of Europe, pioneer farmers used axes like this one to clear areas of land for their fields.

THE FIRST HARVEST
This variety, Einkorn wheat, grows wild in Turkey and Iran, where it was first cultivated.

BACKBREAKING TASK
Cereal crops were harvested with sickles until the coming of the combine harvester in the early part of this century. These three examples represent the three "ages" of prehistory - stone, bronze, and iron.

Leather binding

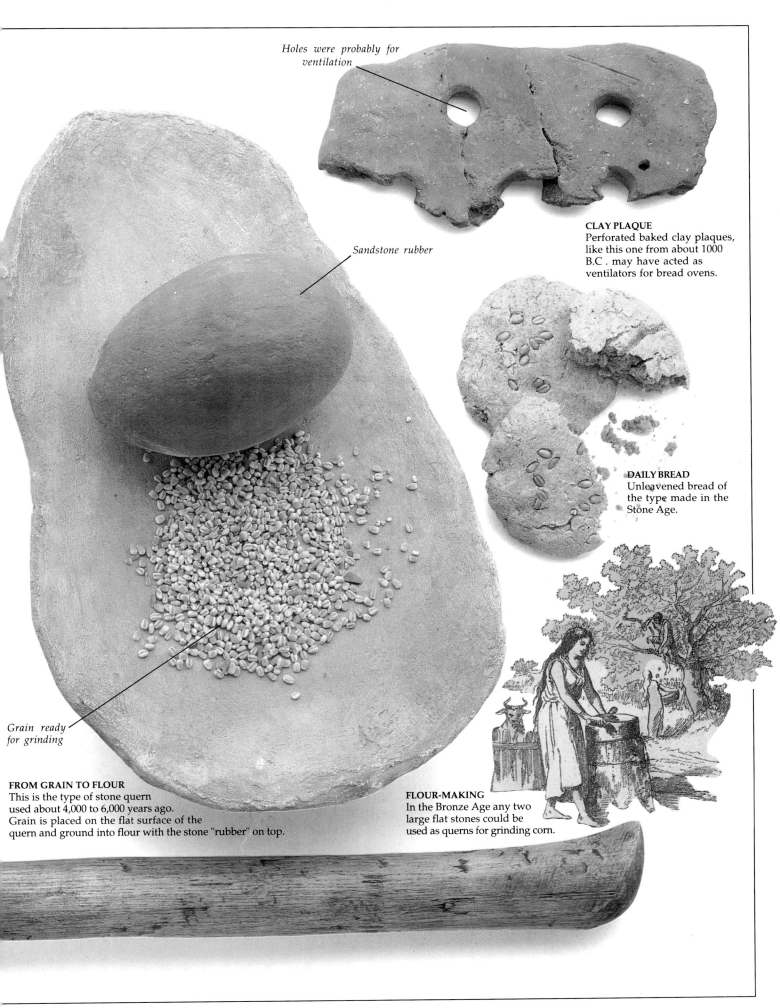

Holes were probably for
ventilation

CLAY PLAQUE
Perforated baked clay plaques,
like this one from about 1000
B.C . may have acted as
ventilators for bread ovens.

Sandstone rubber

DAILY BREAD
Unleavened bread of
the type made in the
Stone Age.

Grain ready
for grinding

FROM GRAIN TO FLOUR
This is the type of stone quern
used about 4,000 to 6,000 years ago.
Grain is placed on the flat surface of the
quern and ground into flour with the stone "rubber" on top.

FLOUR-MAKING
In the Bronze Age any two
large flat stones could be
used as querns for grinding corn.

Clothing and fabrics

THE PEOPLE OF THE ICE AGE were probably the first to wear clothes. They would almost certainly have needed more than their hair to keep warm in the cold conditions, and so they made clothing from the skins and furs of the animals they hunted for food. Stretched and cured, these skins would have provided a very warm covering, and may have been used for shelters as well. The first woollen textiles were probably made in the Near East, where sheep were first domesticated, in the late Stone Age. Spinning and weaving slowly became more popular until, by the Iron Age, quite sophisticated looms were used to weave fine fabrics. Dyes were also used from the Stone Age onward, and these, together with body decoration (pp. 34-35), allowed ancient people to present a bright appearance.

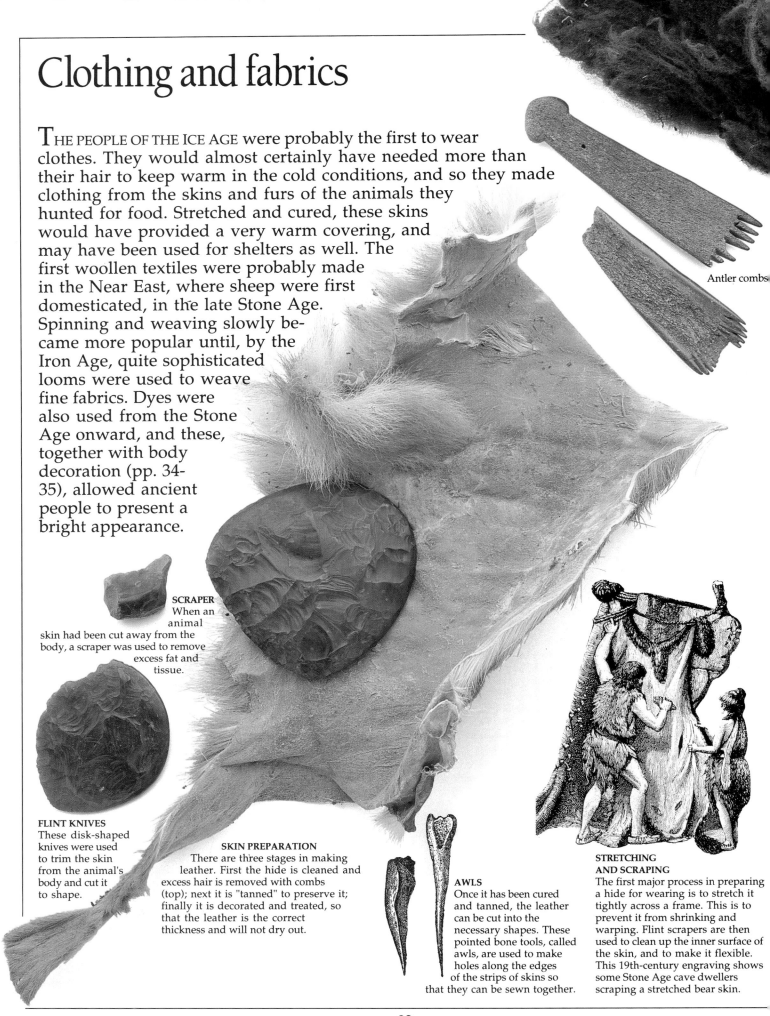

Antler combs

SCRAPER
When an animal skin had been cut away from the body, a scraper was used to remove excess fat and tissue.

FLINT KNIVES
These disk-shaped knives were used to trim the skin from the animal's body and cut it to shape.

SKIN PREPARATION
There are three stages in making leather. First the hide is cleaned and excess hair is removed with combs (top); next it is "tanned" to preserve it; finally it is decorated and treated, so that the leather is the correct thickness and will not dry out.

AWLS
Once it has been cured and tanned, the leather can be cut into the necessary shapes. These pointed bone tools, called awls, are used to make holes along the edges of the strips of skins so that they can be sewn together.

STRETCHING AND SCRAPING
The first major process in preparing a hide for wearing is to stretch it tightly across a frame. This is to prevent it from shrinking and warping. Flint scrapers are then used to clean up the inner surface of the skin, and to make it flexible. This 19th-century engraving shows some Stone Age cave dwellers scraping a stretched bear skin.

RAW WOOL
In ancient times the raw wool was simply plucked off the back of the sheep when it was molting.

Spun wool

Spindle whorl

SPINDLE
The raw wool is twisted around and around the wooden spindle to make a single thread. The clay spindle whorl on the end provides a weight to help the spinning motion.

SPINNING AND WEAVING
This old engraving shows two of the main processes in wool production. The woman in the foreground is spinning the raw wool on the tree into a single thread by twining it around a spindle in her left hand. The man in the background is using a loom to weave the vertical and horizontal threads.

Safflower yellow

Safflower red

WOOL DYES
The safflower, or dyer's thistle, has been used since 2000 B.C.

ANCIENT WOOL
This wool comes from a species of wild sheep which now lives only on the Isle of Soay in the Hebrides islands, off Scotland. It gives us a good idea of what ancient wool looked like. The brown color is quite natural. This wool was spun into a single thread and is now ready to be knitted or woven into a garment or a container.

Neolithic textile

Hole for suspension

Bone shuttle

LOOM
The loom, first invented in the late Stone Age, made it possible to produce woven fabrics for the first time. The frame stretches the vertical woollen threads, and a shuttle is used to weave the horizontal threads in between them.

Recent American backstrap loom

Clay loomweight for stretching threads

Skin deep

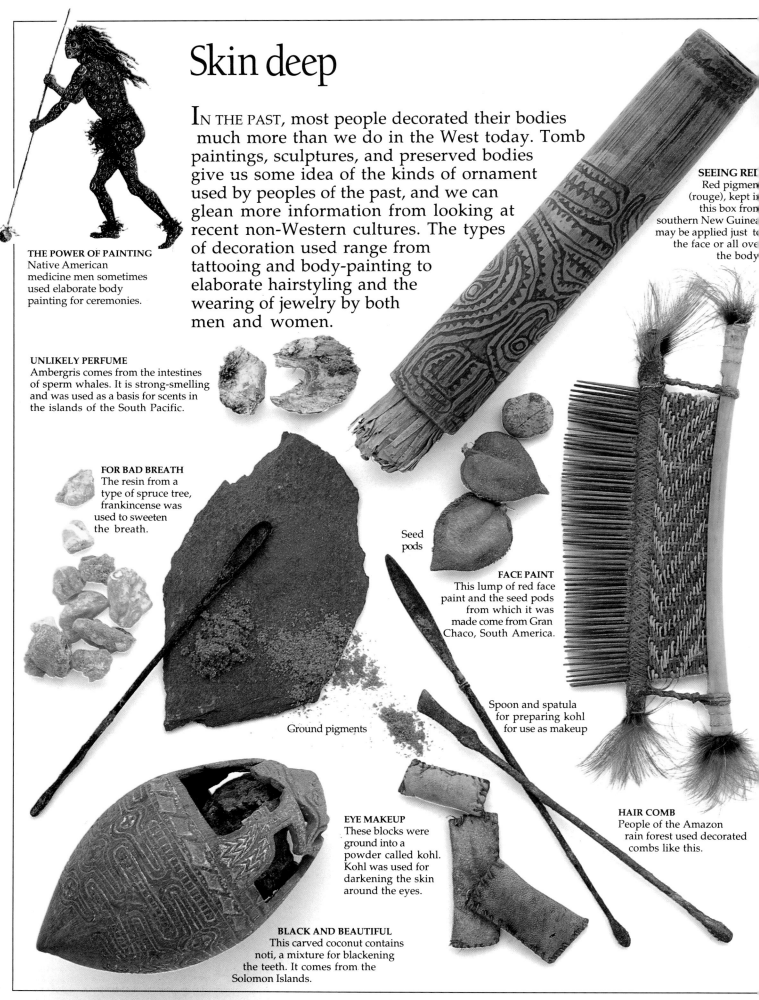

IN THE PAST, most people decorated their bodies much more than we do in the West today. Tomb paintings, sculptures, and preserved bodies give us some idea of the kinds of ornament used by peoples of the past, and we can glean more information from looking at recent non-Western cultures. The types of decoration used range from tattooing and body-painting to elaborate hairstyling and the wearing of jewelry by both men and women.

THE POWER OF PAINTING
Native American medicine men sometimes used elaborate body painting for ceremonies.

SEEING REI
Red pigmen (rouge), kept ir this box from southern New Guinea may be applied just to the face or all ove the body

UNLIKELY PERFUME
Ambergris comes from the intestines of sperm whales. It is strong-smelling and was used as a basis for scents in the islands of the South Pacific.

FOR BAD BREATH
The resin from a type of spruce tree, frankincense was used to sweeten the breath.

Seed pods

FACE PAINT
This lump of red face paint and the seed pods from which it was made come from Gran Chaco, South America.

Ground pigments

Spoon and spatula for preparing kohl for use as makeup

HAIR COMB
People of the Amazon rain forest used decorated combs like this.

EYE MAKEUP
These blocks were ground into a powder called kohl. Kohl was used for darkening the skin around the eyes.

BLACK AND BEAUTIFUL
This carved coconut contains noti, a mixture for blackening the teeth. It comes from the Solomon Islands.

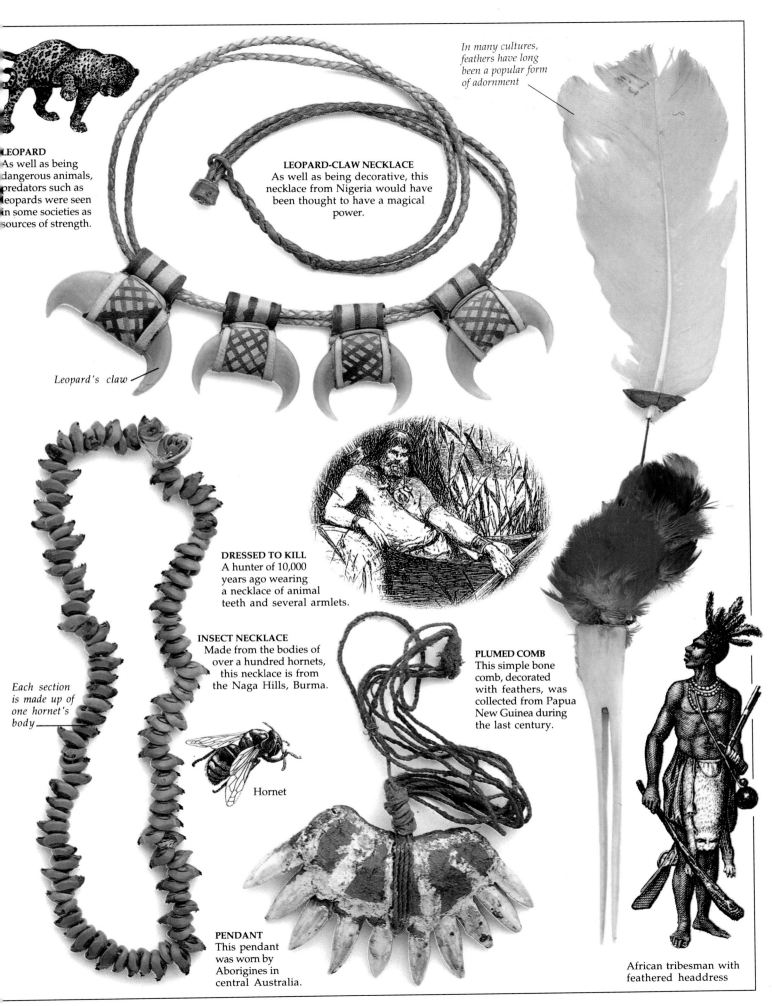

LEOPARD
As well as being dangerous animals, predators such as leopards were seen in some societies as sources of strength.

Leopard's claw

LEOPARD-CLAW NECKLACE
As well as being decorative, this necklace from Nigeria would have been thought to have a magical power.

In many cultures, feathers have long been a popular form of adornment

DRESSED TO KILL
A hunter of 10,000 years ago wearing a necklace of animal teeth and several armlets.

INSECT NECKLACE
Made from the bodies of over a hundred hornets, this necklace is from the Naga Hills, Burma.

Each section is made up of one hornet's body

Hornet

PLUMED COMB
This simple bone comb, decorated with feathers, was collected from Papua New Guinea during the last century.

PENDANT
This pendant was worn by Aborigines in central Australia.

African tribesman with feathered headdress

Magic

AMONG SMALL-SCALE, non-scientific societies, magic and witchcraft are an important part of everyday life. In such a world it is natural to believe that misfortunes such as illness and accidents are caused by powers which take the form of spirits. It is also understandable that people believe that they must consult the spirits in order to find out why some evil has occurred, and what can be done to remedy it. Sometimes it is the job of a particular person - known as a shaman, diviner, or witch doctor - to do this. Usually some sort of offering will need to be made or a ritual performed. Charms are also often worn to protect the wearer from evil. It is likely that the very earliest humans practiced magic, using it to tell them the best times and places to hunt and the best ways to cure illnesses, but little evidence survives. Most of the objects shown here are therefore from recent societies.

This African shaman is using a snake and some bones to foretell the future.

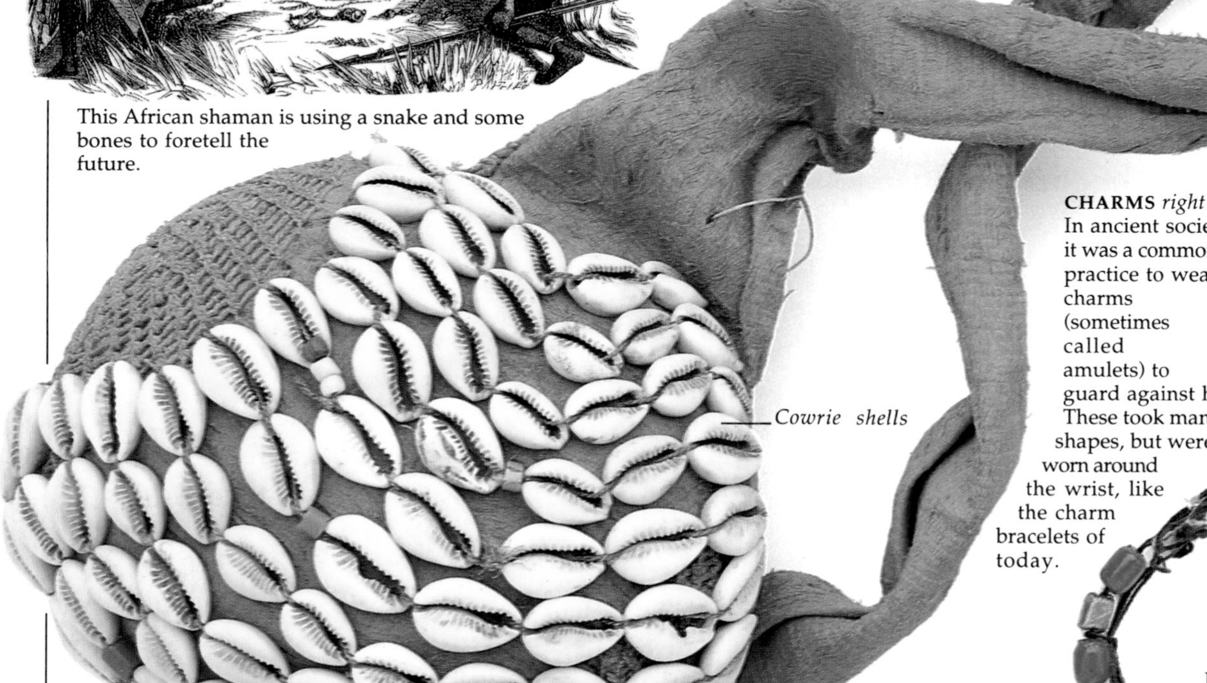

THE DEVIL'S DANCE
This shaman is performing the devil's dance, a religious ceremony of the west coast of Africa. Elaborate costumes, made to look like animals birds, are a common feature of such ceremonies.

FOR FERTILITY
These objects, made of a substance called faience, are Egyptian fertility symbols.

Cowrie shells

CHARMS *right and below*
In ancient societies it was a common practice to wear charms (sometimes called amulets) to guard against harm. These took many shapes, but were often worn around the wrist, like the charm bracelets of today.

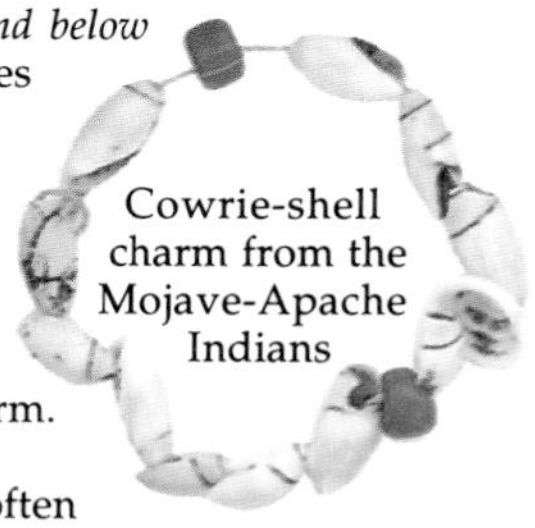

Cowrie-shell charm from the Mojave-Apache Indians

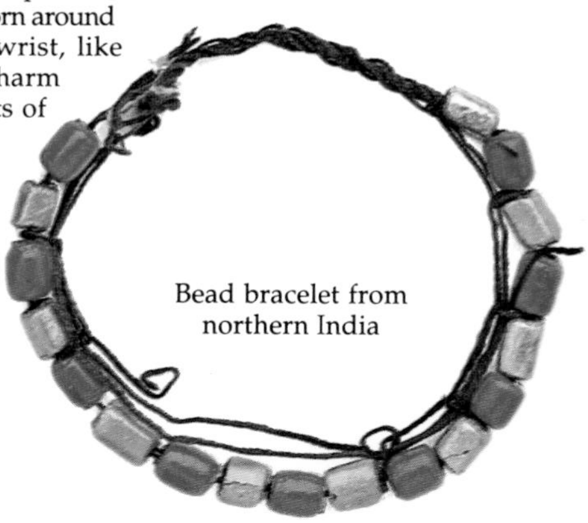

Bead bracelet from northern India

SACRED BUNDLE
This leather bundle from Uganda (East Africa) is covered with cowrie shells. It originally contained various sacred objects used by a diviner.

POWERFUL POPPY
The narcotic effects of opium poppy seeds have been known for thousands of years. In some societies witch doctors used drugs like this to produce trances.

Piece of wood that was floated on the water in the divining bowl

BELLS
In many cases divining is done in a trance-like state along with music and dancing. Drums are used, and bells, like these goat bells from Tanzania, are sometimes rung continuously.

DIVINING BOWL
Divining bowls help people learn the causes of misfortune. This one from Tanzania was filled with water. Objects were then floated on the surface and the shaman figured out the meaning of their movements.

Nutshells

A huge stilt-walking figure in the Apono giant dance

FOR GOOD HEALTH
This little red figure is made up of a combination of wood, bone, leather, cloth, and nuts. It was used among the Nte'va people of central Africa to "watch one's body" - in other words, to protect a person from illness.

DIRECT LINE TO THE SPIRITS
Diviners communicate with a spirit in different ways. Some read messages, some become possessed by the spirit itself, and some speak directly to it through sacred objects like this antelope horn from central Africa.

FISH CHARM
This amulet was worn around the neck as a charm against evil spirits. It was collected in Papua New Guinea and is in the form of a local snapping fish inside a basket.

Death and burial

SINCE THE FIRST Neanderthal burials about 60,000 years ago (see page 18), most people have disposed of their dead formally – by burial, cremation, or mummification. For most of them, death was not the end of their existence, but one stage in a journey. Death has often been seen as the time when the spirit leaves the body to live elsewhere – in heaven, in the landscape, in a tomb, or simply in the household. So in ancient societies, as now, death was looked on as an important stage in a person's existence, and was marked with ceremonies. The treatment of the dead varied greatly from society to society, and was often a complicated procedure. In some ancient societies, a funeral pyre was built and the dead person cremated with sacrificial victims. The bones might then be housed in a burial chamber with rich offerings to accompany the individual in the afterlife. Because such burials were performed deliberately, they are often very well preserved. By study of burial remains, archaeologists can tell a lot about the treatment of the dead in a particular ancient society, and deduce something about the living society, too.

AN EARLY BURIAL
This reconstruction shows the burial of a woman in front of a cave at Les Eyzies, France. The site dates from around 12,000-9000 B.C.

THE PYRAMIDS
This cemetery in Egypt, containing some of the most famous tombs in the world, was built between 2700 and 2500 B.C. The three largest pyramids contained the pharaohs Khufu, Khafra, and Menkaura.

Mummy pits are visible in the foreground

HOUSES OF THE DEAD
"Megaliths" is the name given to a group of monuments consisting of huge slabs of stone. Some of them seem never to have housed human remains, but were simply monuments, while others contained the remains of dozens of jumbled-up skeletons. These examples are around five thousand years old.

The entrance to a chambered tomb, the Cairn of Dowth, Ireland

Barley

Jujube

Melon

Mimusop

FOOD FOR THE DEAD
These seeds from the burial of the Egyptian pharaoh Tutankhamun were recently found in an old box at Kew Gardens, England. They had been recovered during excavation and sent for analysis, but lay forgotten for 46 years. They are the remains of food offerings, and tell us much about the plants and diet available at the time.

Cremation urn

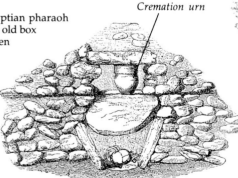

BURIAL MOUND
This engraving shows a skeleton from c. 2000 B.C. buried in a chamber covered by a stone slab. Above it, a cremation in an urn has been buried at a later date.

A megalith consisting of six uprights and a covering slab, at Gaulstown, Ireland

This type of pot was often used both in the home and in cremations.

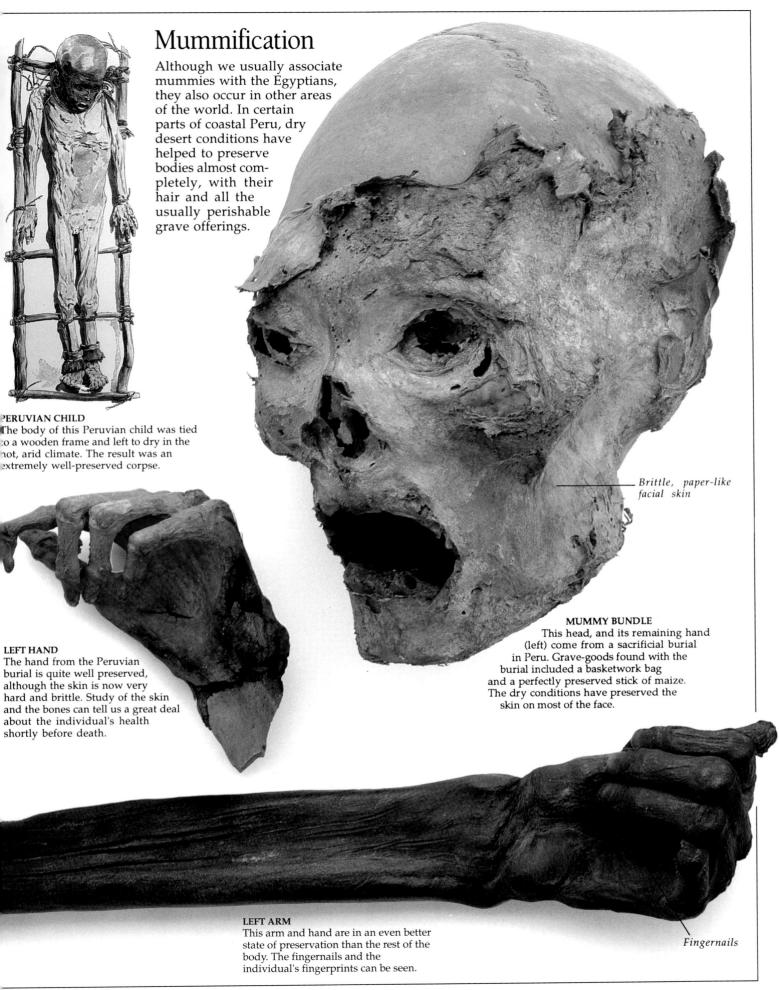

Mummification

Although we usually associate mummies with the Egyptians, they also occur in other areas of the world. In certain parts of coastal Peru, dry desert conditions have helped to preserve bodies almost completely, with their hair and all the usually perishable grave offerings.

PERUVIAN CHILD
The body of this Peruvian child was tied to a wooden frame and left to dry in the hot, arid climate. The result was an extremely well-preserved corpse.

Brittle, paper-like facial skin

LEFT HAND
The hand from the Peruvian burial is quite well preserved, although the skin is now very hard and brittle. Study of the skin and the bones can tell us a great deal about the individual's health shortly before death.

MUMMY BUNDLE
This head, and its remaining hand (left) come from a sacrificial burial in Peru. Grave-goods found with the burial included a basketwork bag and a perfectly preserved stick of maize. The dry conditions have preserved the skin on most of the face.

LEFT ARM
This arm and hand are in an even better state of preservation than the rest of the body. The fingernails and the individual's fingerprints can be seen.

Fingernails

Ancient writing

THE FIRST WRITING gradually developed in Mesopotamia (in part of modern Iraq) and was used to record trading deals. At first, pictures of the objects being exchanged were simply drawn on tokens; later, symbols were used to represent ideas. By about 3500 B.C., the actual sounds of speech (either whole words or syllables) were written down on clay tablets using a stylus. This type of script is known as cuneiform. The idea of writing spread around the Old World, and by about 1000 B.C. the Phoenicians had invented an alphabet. Writing was also independently invented in other places. In China it first appears engraved on bones to record military affairs and the deeds of kings. In Central America, the Maya used hieroglyphs, most of which have only recently been "translated," to make astronomical records and to list royal dynasties. In all these ancient societies writing was restricted to the upper classes because it was a source of knowledge and power.

CUNEIFORM TABLET
The earliest form of writing, known as cuneiform, consists of signs made by pressing a wedge-ended stylus into a slab of wet clay. This is an account table from Mesopotamia, dating from c. 3400 B.C.

Impression

Seal

CYLINDER SEAL
This was used in early Mesopotamia to seal documents. Cylinder seals bore the name of their owner, and were simply rolled over the moist clay of a tablet to make a distinctive impression. This one is over 5,000 years old.

FOUNDATION STONE
This four-thousand-year-old brick cone, from the famous Sumerian city of Ur, was placed in a mudbrick wall to record the foundation of a building.

Cuneiform signs made with a wedge-ended stylus

Seal

Impression

BOAR SEAL *left*
Seals were made from a variety of stones, some of them precious, and had a number of different forms. This one, dating from about 3400 B.C., takes the form of a wild boar.

BULL SEAL *right*
The great Indus civilization of northern India and Pakistan reached its peak between 2300 and 1750 B.C. Like the Sumerians, the Indus people also used a form of writing, and recorded trading deals with seals. This stone seal, showing a bull, is typical of the period.

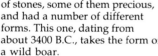

Seal

Impression

Mayan writing stamped on pottery

Mayan writing engraved on bone

Painted Mayan writing

MAYAN WRITING
For generations, scholars were baffled by the pictorial script of the Maya. It bears no resemblance to any other known writing. The first simple bars and dots of the calendar were translated in 1880, but for nearly a hundred years it was thought that Mayan writing was used only for recording the calendar and for astronomical calculations. It was not till the 1960s that researchers found that some glyphs referred to the kings and their exploits. Now nearly 80 percent are have been decoded and a history of the Maya is being uncovered.

Mayan characters

MAYAN TOMB SLAB *above*
The writing on this stone relief identifies it as showing the ruler "Shield Jaguar" with his wife, Lady Xoc, kneeling before him and ritually drawing blood from her tongue.

Writing in Egypt

The idea of writing probably traveled to Egypt from western Asia, but the script itself was invented locally. Three basic kinds were used. The official script used for inscriptions was hieroglyphic; for writing on papyrus with pens, priests used a form called hieratic; a simpler kind, called demotic, was for everyday use.

SCRIBES AT WORK *above*
Armies of scribes were vital to the functioning of ancient Egypt's complex society. They ensured that records were kept, business conducted, and taxes collected.

HIEROGLYPHICS *left*
Hieroglyphic is a kind of script where the symbols stand for parts of words. It was developed about 3000 B.C. and, unlike cuneiform, was used for historical records, and on tombs and temples.

Man

Two

On

Rich

CHINESE CHARACTERS *above*
The Chinese script is the oldest writing still in use in the world. In the Bronze Age Shang period a form was used from around 1300 B.C. which is still recognizably related to modern Chinese. In 221 B.C. the Ch'in state brought in a standard script to replace all the regional variations that had developed, and this is still used today.

PAPYRUS *above*
Early paper was made from this reed.

Bronzeworking

BRONZE IS A MIXTURE of copper and tin. Its use became widespread in Europe around 2000 B.C. Copper had been used to make metal objects before this date, but these were usually only ornamental as copper and tin are too soft to make useful tools or weapons. By adding 10 percent tin to the copper, a far harder alloy could be produced, and one which could be cast in many different shapes. It could take a sharp edge and be resharpened or melted down and recast when it was worn. These qualities made it a very useful metal. Most bronze objects (from swords to brooches, knives to pins) were made by casting - pouring the molten metal into a mold and allowing it to cool and set. Sheet-metal items such as shields were hammered into shape. While stone is abundant locally, copper ores are not common in Europe, and tin is rare, so the shift to bronze brought widespread social changes. Prospectors and miners appeared long-distance trade in metal ingots developed, and central trading areas came into being. Control of the trade was a great source of power, and large fortified settlements grew up which dominated the trade routes and served as centers of manufacturing.

MELTING DOWN THE ORE
Copper and tin, the usual ingredients of bronze, occur as ores which have to be mined from the earth. In order to obtain the metal, the ore is heated to a high temperature to melt the metal and separate it from the rock. This process is known as smelting. To produce bronze, solid copper and tin ingots are melted together to form a bronze ingot. This in turn can be remelted and poured into a mold.

A PRECIOUS METAL
The liquid bronze was poured into the mold. The skill required to cast objects in this way, together with the specialist equipment needed, made bronze items particularly valuable. People had to be prepared to barter with the bronzeworker to obtain the things they wanted.

BRONZE DEBRIS
When copper and tin ores are melted together, the resulting alloy is collected in the bottom of the melting pot in bowl-shaped ingots. The debris on the left shows part of the outline of one of these.

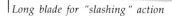
Long blade for "slashing" action

Original golden color

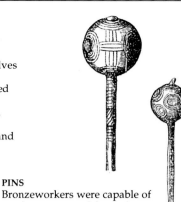

STONE MOLD

This is one section of a two-piece mold used for casting round-headed pins. When the two halves were joined together, molten bronze was poured in through holes at the pointed end of each pin. This mold is from Mörigen, Switzerland, and dates from c. 1000 B.C.

PINS

Bronzeworkers were capable of producing quite elaborately decorated objects, as these pins from Switzerland show. The different types of patterns on pins like this can give archaeologists useful clues to the origins of bronze items and the people who made them.

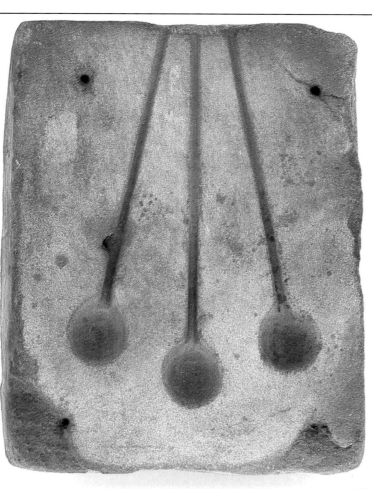

END PRODUCT

This is the type of bronze pin that would have been produced using the stone mold shown.

MOMENT OF TRUTH

These bronzeworkers are casting swords whose handles are similar to to the one shown below. The person in the foreground is examining a sword to check that it is free of flaws. The mold used in this process has an extra channel to pour the metal through. When the cast had set and the mold was opened up, the excess bronze found in this channel was removed. Extra metal where the two halves of the mold joined together was also removed or smoothed down.

READY FOR RECYCLING

These axes, dating from c. 750 B.C., are damaged. They may have formed part of the stock-in-trade of a bronzeworker, ready to melt down and recycle.

Decorated hilt

TWO SWORDS

These swords would have been cast using the methods shown on this page. The upper sword is from Avignon, France, and the lower is from Denmark. The Danish sword has been cleaned to show its original gold color; the French sword has the dull, aged color of most ancient bronze objects.

The beauties of bronze

BRONZE TOOLS AND WEAPONS are not much sharper than flint ones, so the original reason for developing bronzeworking around 2000 B.C. probably had to do with social status. When it is new, bronze is a shiny gold color and can be richly decorated. It soon became a valuable substance, and one which was ideally suited for showing a person's wealth and power. When it was first invented it was popular among the upper classes for ornamental objects such as jewelry. It was also used to make tools and weapons, which themselves were often impressively decorated. When iron became widespread in Europe, around 750 B.C., it was used for the heavier tools and weapons, thus freeing the bronze-workers to concentrate on producing luxury items and decorative objects, like jewelry, ornaments, and horse harness decorations.

WHAT ARE THEY DOING?
This mysterious engraving is taken from the design on a bronze vessel found in the Tyrol, Austria.

PENDANT
This beaten bronze pendant was probably suspended on a chain worn around the neck. The type of simple bronze chain in use at this time is shown on the opposite page.

Pin is shown actual size

Harness mounts found in Norfolk, England

HORSEMANSHIP
In the late Bronze Age the use of horses became widespread.

TWEEZERS
Like today, tweezers were probably used in the Bronze Age for pulling out hairs.

Typical serpentine ornament

Razors were made of beaten metal, and engraved with patterns

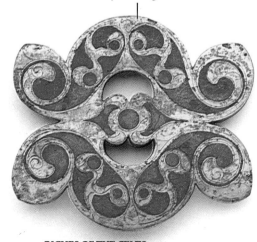

RICHES OF THE CELTS
The chariots of the aristocratic Celtic horsemen of the late Iron Age (c. 100 B.C.-A.D. 100) were decorated with fine metalwork. Here, red enamel highlights the pattern.

BRIDLE SIDEPIECE
This part of a horse harness was found in Cambridge, England.

FOR USE AND ORNAMENT
These elegant razors were found in Denmark. Human bodies, preserved in the peat in the same area, were clean shaven; people no doubt used razors similar to these.

Bronze Age pin, fashionable after 2000 B.C.

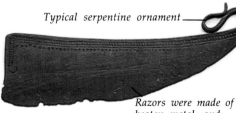

Fastening held closed by tension of ring

SUNFLOWER PINS
These pins are so named because of the position of their carefully crafted heads, which would have shone brightly on the clothing of the wearer. They date from c. 1200 B.C.

Flower-shaped head

WORN BY THE POWERFUL
The neck ring or "torque" was an important status symbol in the Celtic-speaking world of the Iron Age. Torques were also worn by warriors as a protective charm. This one, from the 6th century B.C., is made from a single piece of twisted bronze.

AROUND THE WAIST
One of a series of ornaments attached to a belt, this boss was made from a thin sheet of bronze. The decorations were hammered upward from the back, using a technique called *repoussé*. This boss is from Auvernier, Switzerland.

Simple bent-metal link

SWISS JEWELRY
This chain may have formed part of a necklace. It was found in a Bronze Age village by a Swiss lake.

BRACELET
Some of the richest bracelets from the Bronze Age took the form of metal spirals.

WOMEN'S BELT BOSS
These bosses have been found with many female burials in Denmark.

ALL DRESSED UP
Bronze Age women would have worn dresses like the one shown in this engraving.

Found in Denmark, this is the pattern for a woman's jacket.

45

A Bronze Age warrior

THROUGHOUT THE WESTERN WORLD a more obviously warlike society was evolving around 2,200-700 B.C., the time of the Bronze Age in Europe. This period gives our first evidence of individual armed combat and of societies in which the warrior and his skills were valued. The weapons used were spears, for attacking enemies at a distance, and swords and axes, proving that hand-to-hand fighting took place. The high position of warriors during the Bronze Age is shown by the richness of their personal ornaments (which included jewelry such as bangles and pins with large ornate heads) and the elaborate decoration on some of their weapons.

BANGLE
This intricately engraved bangle is from Auvernier, Switzerland, and dates from c. 1200 B.C.

Found in Switzerland, these pins date from c. 1000 B.C.

BEFORE BUTTONS
Pins were used for fastening clothing before the invention of buttons.

THE FIRST KNIGHTS
Horseback riding became widespread in the late Bronze Age, and men used slashing swords for fighting.

FOR FOOD OR FIGHTING?
Small knives, like this one from Switzerland, were probably used for cutting food rather than as weapons.

STATUS SYMBOLS
Spears were symbols of the warrior in the Bronze Age, and were often very ornate.

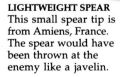

LIGHTWEIGHT SPEAR
This small spear tip is from Amiens, France. The spear would have been thrown at the enemy like a javelin.

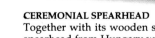
Socket for wooden shaft

CEREMONIAL SPEARHEAD
Together with its wooden shaft, this massive socketed spearhead from Hungary would have made a weapon over 6 ft (2m) long. It was almost certainly for ceremonial use rather than for battle.

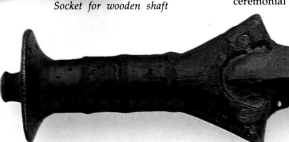

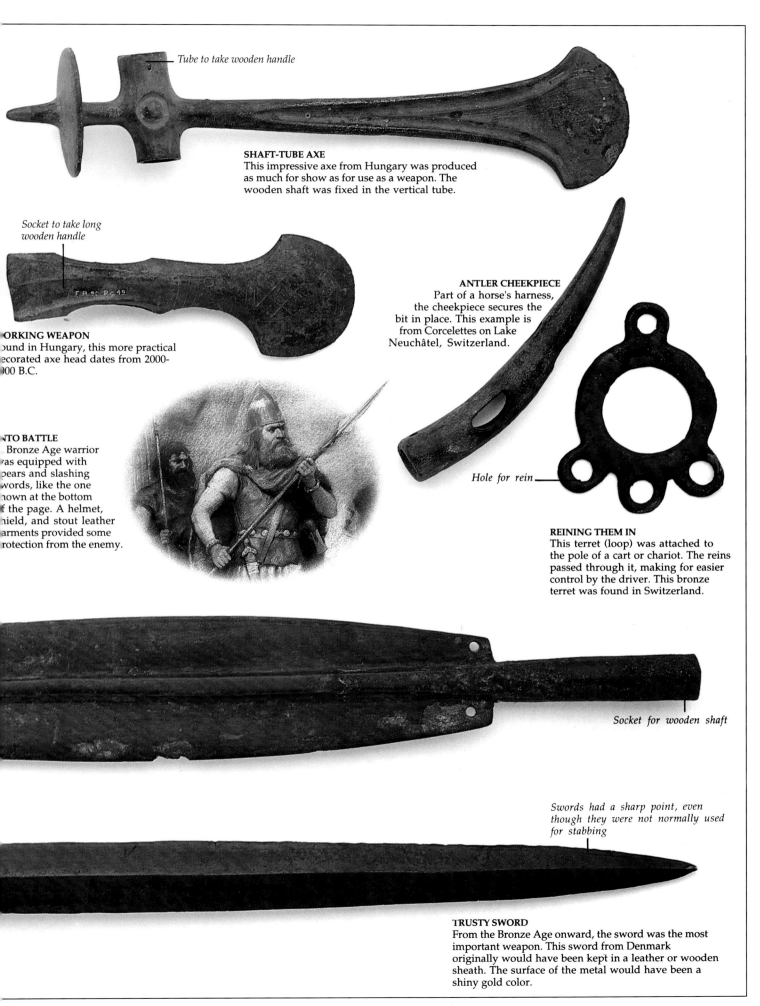

Tube to take wooden handle

SHAFT-TUBE AXE
This impressive axe from Hungary was produced
as much for show as for use as a weapon. The
wooden shaft was fixed in the vertical tube.

*Socket to take long
wooden handle*

ANTLER CHEEKPIECE
Part of a horse's harness,
the cheekpiece secures the
bit in place. This example is
from Corcelettes on Lake
Neuchâtel, Switzerland.

...ORKING WEAPON
...ound in Hungary, this more practical
...ecorated axe head dates from 2000-
...00 B.C.

...NTO BATTLE
... Bronze Age warrior
...as equipped with
...ears and slashing
...words, like the one
...hown at the bottom
...f the page. A helmet,
...hield, and stout leather
...arments provided some
...rotection from the enemy.

Hole for rein

REINING THEM IN
This terret (loop) was attached to
the pole of a cart or chariot. The reins
passed through it, making for easier
control by the driver. This bronze
terret was found in Switzerland.

Socket for wooden shaft

*Swords had a sharp point, even
though they were not normally used
for stabbing*

TRUSTY SWORD
From the Bronze Age onward, the sword was the most
important weapon. This sword from Denmark
originally would have been kept in a leather or wooden
sheath. The surface of the metal would have been a
shiny gold color.

Iron Age finery

SOME OF THE FINEST decorated personal items of the Iron Age are made of bronze, because iron was reserved for heavy tools and weapons. Unlike iron, bronze could be cast into complex shapes and be highly decorated. Classical writers report that the Celts of Iron Age Europe were fond of adornment, including body painting, elaborate hairstyles, and jewelry (pp. 34-35). A characteristic ornament was a silver neck ring called a torque (p. 45), symbolic of high social rank. Some fighting men went into battle naked except for their torque, trusting in its protective power. Over their trousers and tunics men and women wore woollen cloaks fastened with brooches, sometimes of elaborate design. In graves, it is usually only these that survive to indicate the sort of clothing that was worn. The upper classes would adorn their horses with fine harnesses covered with disks, studs, and bells.

SPECTACLE-BROOCH
This type of brooch is so called because of its shape. It is made from a single twisted piece of wire and would have had a pin at the back. It is from Carinthia in Austria and dates from between 1000 and 800 B.C.

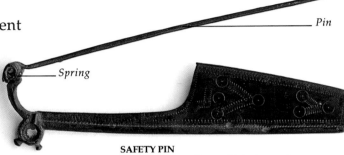

Pin

Spring

SAFETY PIN
Brooches were the prehistoric versions of safety pins. They were used in exactly the same way as they are today, for joining clothes together. This Hungarian brooch dates from c. 50 B.C.

Spring

Pin

Glass disk

A MARK OF RANK
A composite bow made up of glass disks makes this an especially striking brooch. It would have been quite a rarity and was probably worn by someone of high rank. It is from Italy, and dates from between 800 and 700 B.C.

CHIEFTAIN
In this rather romantic engraving, the nineteenth-century illustrator has tried to combine all the elements known about Iron Age dress into one picture. The chieftain has a horned helmet and a bushy mustache (although pigtails are not reported!). His cloak is fastened by a brooch, and he is wearing a shiny breastplate for battle. Under his short tunic he wears trousers which are ideal for riding a horse. The woman has an elaborate girdle, from which a dagger hangs. She is presenting the chieftain with a drinking horn filled with beer taken from the decorated pail in the foreground.

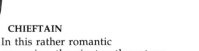

FIRM FASTENINGS
Two more examples from northern Europe show the skill that Iron Age metalworkers could focus on these simple fasteners. The strong, sprung pins themselves are clearly visible.

FOLLOWING THE PATTERN
This bronze pendant with enameled decoration is from a Saxon burial slightly later than the other objects on this page. But the curves and circles used in its decoration show how this style of art continued to be used in northern Europe.

FOR MEN AND WOMEN
Bracelets like this were commonly worn on the arms - probably by both male and female members of the household. This one was found near Cambridge, England, and was made c. 50 B.C. Its delicate pattern would have been more striking when it was new.

A CLEAN SHAVE
This razor, now about 2500 years old, is less ornate than some of the razors of the Bronze Age (pp. 44-45) but it is highly functional: it would have been just as sharp as any modern straight razor. It comes from Cambridge, England.

Decorated back of mirror

WELL SHOD
Iron Age horseshoes are sometimes found. Their form is similar to those in use today.

FAIREST OF THEM ALL
Some of the most beautiful objects that have survived from the Iron Age are mirrors. This one is decorated in the distinctive, swirling style of Celtic art. The back is shown in the photograph; the other side would be highly polished to give a reflection. Mirrors like this are rare and no doubt belonged to the wealthiest families.

BOAR HUNT
Iron horseshoes similar to the one above can be seen in this old engraving. The fine trappings that decorate the horses of the huntsmen are also clearly shown. The large disks are made of bronze and are known as phalerae. In the Iron Age the boar was hunted for sport as well as for its meat.

Life in the Iron Age

THE FIRST REALLY SKILLED IRONWORKERS were the Hittites, who lived in what is now central Turkey. They perfected the techniques of smelting ore and making iron objects around 1500 B.C. The Hittites guarded the secrets of ironworking carefully, but when their empire was overthrown their knowledge spread across Europe, where the Iron Age began around 1100 B.C. By this time, Europe was quite densely settled with small farming communities. Although the society as a whole was ruled by a warrior class (pp. 52-53), life for the majority of people consisted of an unending round of farming activities, basically unchanged for generations. Settlements were still mainly family-based, and even small children played a full part in daily work. Many iron objects (especially tools) have survived from this period, as well as a large amount of pottery, and decorative objects made of bronze.

BOG PEOPLE
Bodies preserved in the airless conditions of European peat bogs give us a glimpse of the actual people of the Iron Age. Tollund Man, discovered in Denmark, dates from about 210 B.C.

INSTANT PATTERNS
Later Saxon potters made similar shaped pots to those of the Iron Age, but decorated them with punches.

Punch for cross pattern

Punch for circle pattern

BRONZE BOWL
In the Iron Age many of the more decorative and high-status objects were in fact made of bronze, a material that looked shiny and could be engraved with detailed patterns. Fine bronze imported tableware like this bowl was highly prized by many upper-class families in northern Europe, who were eager to adopt Mediterranean customs.

Engraved decoration

Shape made by hammering out bronze

STATUS SYMBOL?
In the last hundred years before the Roman invasion of Britain, wealthy people developed a taste for fine pottery. Beakers like this one were imported from Europe in large numbers.

This smaller decorated pot was found in a British Iron Age burial mound.

IRON TOOLS

The introduction of iron into Europe provided an ideal material for making sturdy tools and weapons; iron was also more widely available than the tin and copper needed to make bronze. Unfortunately, iron corrodes (rots away) much more quickly than bronze, so most of the items that have survived are in poorer condition than bronze objects of the same period.

KNIFE

This small iron-bladed knife has a handle made of antler. Although the blade is corroded, the handle is very well preserved because of favorable soil conditions.

Iron blade

Antler handle

Iron blade

Iron blade

Antler handle

Serrated (notched) cutting edge

HARVESTER

This reaping hook has the same sickle-shaped design that was used for gathering hay or crops throughout the prehistoric period (pp. 30-31). This example has an antler handle.

CUTTER

A wooden handle made this iron saw almost as easy to use as its modern counterpart.

Holes for attaching wooden handle

FORGING AHEAD

In this old engraving of blacksmiths at work, the method of shaping a piece of hot metal by hammering it is clearly shown. In the background, more iron is being heated in a furnace.

TONGS

Iron was worked by beating it into shape while it was red hot. The metal was held in large tongs, like these from Norfolk, England.

Men of iron

LANCE HEAD
This unusually shaped object is made of wrought iron.

Human head

WE KNOW ABOUT the Celtic-speaking peoples who lived north of the Alps from about 500 B.C. through the reports of Greek and Roman historians. They describe barbarian people with customs quite different from their own, such as human sacrifice and head-hunting. These tribes were ruled by warriors, who placed a high value on their heroic lifestyle, which included feasting and drinking, reciting poetry, singing, horseback riding, and, of course, skill in battle. The Celts were as concerned with scaring their enemies as with actually fighting them. We know this because of the fearsome appearance of their arms, armor, and other possessions.

A nineteenth-century illustration of a Celtic warrior chief in battle

HEAD IN HAND
The handle of this dagger is shaped like a human figure. It dates from 100 B.C.-A.D. 100.

LETHAL LONDONER
This is a fine early dagger from c. 500 B.C., found in the Thames River, London.

SHINY SHEATH
Made from thin sheets of bronze riveted together, this sheath has a birch-bark lining.

HELMET FOR A HERO
This bronze helmet would have belonged to a high-ranking warrior, and was probably for display rather than battle.

Hollow horn made of riveted sheet bronze

19th-century illustration of Iron Age warfare

Oak lining

Diameter of tankard is about 7 in (175 mm)

Loops for fastening leather interior

AXLE HUB
This decoration was attached to the axle of a light chariot of the type used against the Roman army invading Britain.

WHAT YOUR RIGHT ARM IS FOR...
Drinking was popular with the warriors, as this 4 pint (2.3 liter) bronze vessel shows. The drink was probably a beer made from barley.

BRONZE TERRET
This was fixed to the yoke of a chariot (p. 47).

BIT BETWEEN THE TEETH
The bit is inserted in the horse's mouth and controlled by pulling on the reins. It has an iron core covered with decorated bronze.

IRON SWORD *below*
This sword would have had a decorated sheath of leather or wood. It dates from c. 150 B.C.-A.D. 50.

Hilt (handle) would have been covered in wood, bone, or leather

Ancient China

For thousands of years, Chinese civilization evolved with little or no contact with the Western world, and the Chinese made several independent inventions, such as farming and writing. The first stone-using agricultural communities were followed by a variety of societies, most of which survived by farming a range of crops including rice and millet. True civilization dates from c.1500 B.C. with the Bronze Age Shang Dynasty. At this time China was a loose group of states which were gradually joined together. Between 500 and 200 B.C., the two principal states, Ch'u and Ch'in, battled for power. Under the victorious Ch'in and the later Han (206 B.C.-A.D. 220) an empire of 60 million people prospered. The Great Wall was built, and standard systems of writing, laws, and taxes were created.

CHINESE NOBLEMEN
These men belonged to the court of Emperor Tscheu-Sin, c. 1150 B.C.

RARE AND DEADLY *above*
The halberd is a weapon mounted at right-angles on a tall wooden shaft, kind of like a 15th century pike. This halberd of white jade is over 3,000 years old. It was probably both for battle and for ceremonial use, especially for sacrifices.

RITUAL HALBERD
This sacrificial halberd is a good example of the superb bronzeworking of the Shang Dynasty (1523-1027 B.C.). This skill arose from local roots, although there was also some outside influence from the West. With its ornate patterns, this halberd would have played an important role in rituals, for both human and animal sacrifices.

STONE TOOLS
Like their counterparts in Europe, the first Chinese farmers had to clear forests with stone axes and till the soil with mattocks (pickaxes). Both of these tools have similar shapes the world over. In China, however, they were used to cultivate different crops - millet in the north and rice in the south.

Stone mattock

Polished stone axe from Shansi, northern China

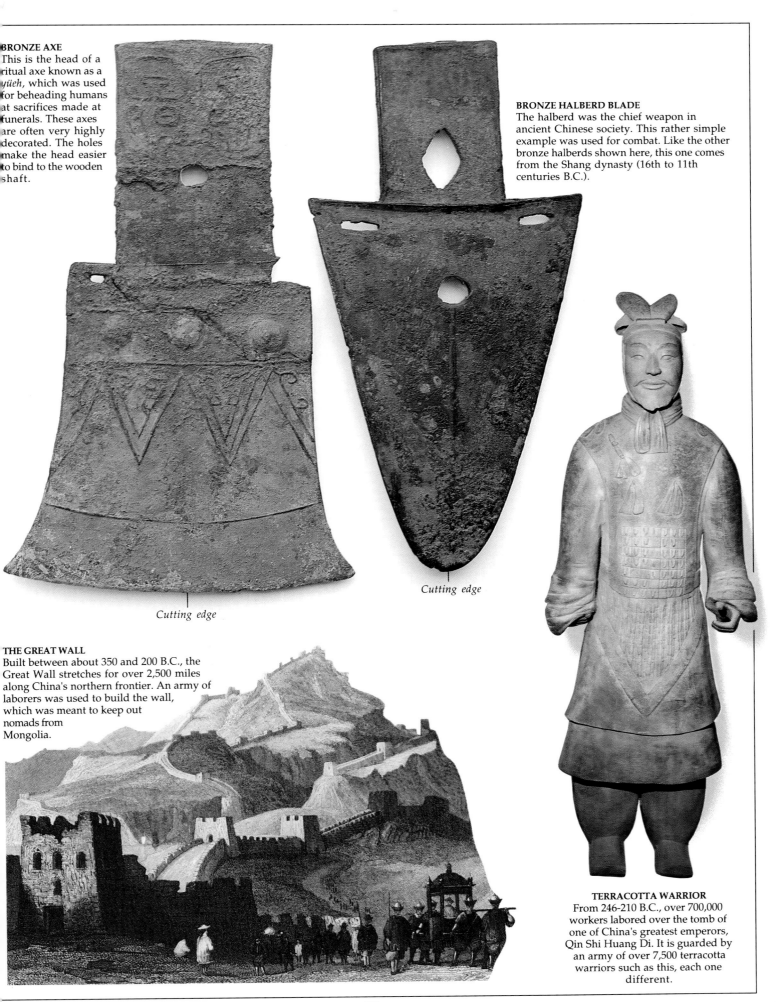

BRONZE AXE
This is the head of a ritual axe known as a *yüeh*, which was used for beheading humans at sacrifices made at funerals. These axes are often very highly decorated. The holes make the head easier to bind to the wooden shaft.

BRONZE HALBERD BLADE
The halberd was the chief weapon in ancient Chinese society. This rather simple example was used for combat. Like the other bronze halberds shown here, this one comes from the Shang dynasty (16th to 11th centuries B.C.).

Cutting edge

Cutting edge

THE GREAT WALL
Built between about 350 and 200 B.C., the Great Wall stretches for over 2,500 miles along China's northern frontier. An army of laborers was used to build the wall, which was meant to keep out nomads from Mongolia.

TERRACOTTA WARRIOR
From 246-210 B.C., over 700,000 workers labored over the tomb of one of China's greatest emperors, Qin Shi Huang Di. It is guarded by an army of over 7,500 terracotta warriors such as this, each one different.

Small change

GOD OF RICHES
This relief shows the goddess Demeter and her son Plutus, the god of riches in Greek mythology.

WE USUALLY THINK OF MONEY as consisting of coins and bank notes, but anything used when making payments can be called money. In ancient societies many different things, from small shells to huge stones punched with holes, have been used to make payments, and some of these types of currency are still used today. The most common way of making a payment was originally barter, in which one item was exchanged for another. For many societies without currency, gift-giving was very important and some valued objects were regularly passed around as gifts. Other large or rare forms of money, such as cattle or perforated stones, might be given for payments of a social kind, such as compensation for a person killed, or in exchange for a woman taken as a bride. Even after standard coinage was developed about 2,500 years ago, this social use of money continued; many examples shown here come from recent societies.

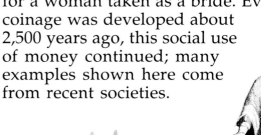

Rice

CHINESE CURRENCY
In China, coinage was invented quite independently of the Western world, but later, in the fifth century B.C. The first coins looked like tiny knives; later ones were round.

Knife shape is common in early Chinese currency

TRADE IN RICE
As well as using coinage, the Chinese used food, especially rice, to pay for different kinds of goods.

DOGS' TEETH
This necklace from Papua New Guinea is made up of the canine teeth of dogs, threaded on to a leather thong. Its function was the same as the larger one from Africa (above right).

FOR CARRYING CASH
Cowrie shells have been used as money since prehistoric times. This wickerwork purse for carrying them comes from the Congo, central Africa.

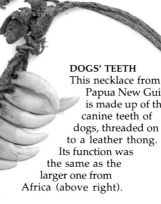

Quartz pebbles

STONE NECKLACE
This is not simply an item of personal jewelry: the beads were also used to make payments. This necklace, from Ghana (Africa), is made of perforated quartz pebbles.

GAMBLING COUNTERS
Gambling is as old as money itself, and so gambling counters have a long history. These decorated porcelain counters are from Hong Kong and are nearly 2,000 years old.

Stone is about 2 ft (60 cm) in diameter. The largest were up to 13 ft (4 m) across.

Disk is about 9 in (23 cm) in diameter

Cowrie shells from India

TOO BIG FOR THE POCKET
In the Naya hills of Tibet, high up in the Himalayas, metal disks like this were used as currency. Known as *laya*, this particular example is rather small, and had half the value of the more usual large size

MONEY STONE
From Yap Island, north of New Guinea, limestone disks known as *fei* were used as currency.

GREEK COIN
This coin is from Aegina, Greece. The turtle is the symbol of the city.

Central Americans

PEOPLE FIRST CAME TO THE AMERICAS about 13,000 years ago, when hunters followed big game across a bridge of land that joined Siberia to Alaska during the Ice Age. These people began to move south and to develop without contact with the Old World. By 6,000 BC, corn was being grown in Central America (in Mexico, Guatemala, El Salvador, and Belize), and gradually a number of spectacular civilizations developed. These had large ceremonial centers with temples, palaces, and markets. Many practiced a ritual ball game in specially laid out courts. Some had an elaborate religion that included human sacrifice, and used a kind of picture-writing that is only just being deciphered. These civilizations were at their height between AD 300 and 900, after which they collapsed. They were followed by a succession of empires, including the Aztec empire, which was found and overthrown by the Spanish in 1519.

WHISTLE
This whistle is made of pottery. It comes from Guatemala and is thought to represent a stylized bird.

POTTERY
This piece of decorated pottery, dating to around A.D. 500, comes from Teotihuacán, at the time the largest city in Mexico.

CALENDAR STONE
The calendar was of great importance in the daily life of the Aztecs. Each day had its own good or evil tidings, and each month its special ceremonies. There were two different years, of 260 and 365 days, both based on a 20-day cycle.

TEMPLE CARVINGS
This is a typical example of Classic period temple sculpture, showing animals, people, symbolic twisted serpents, and images of gods. It comes from a temple at Xochicalco.

STONE HEAD
From Seibal in Guatemala, this sandstone head may have decorated a temple. It dates from the Classic period, A.D. 300-900.

FUNERARY URN *right*
In the Oaxaca Valley of Mexico, the Monte Albán civilization flourished from A.D. 300-900. The dead were buried in tombs with brightly painted walls. Inside the tomb, their ashes would be housed in pottery urns such as this one. It represents a god sitting cross-legged, with an elaborate headdress containing the symbol by which he is known.

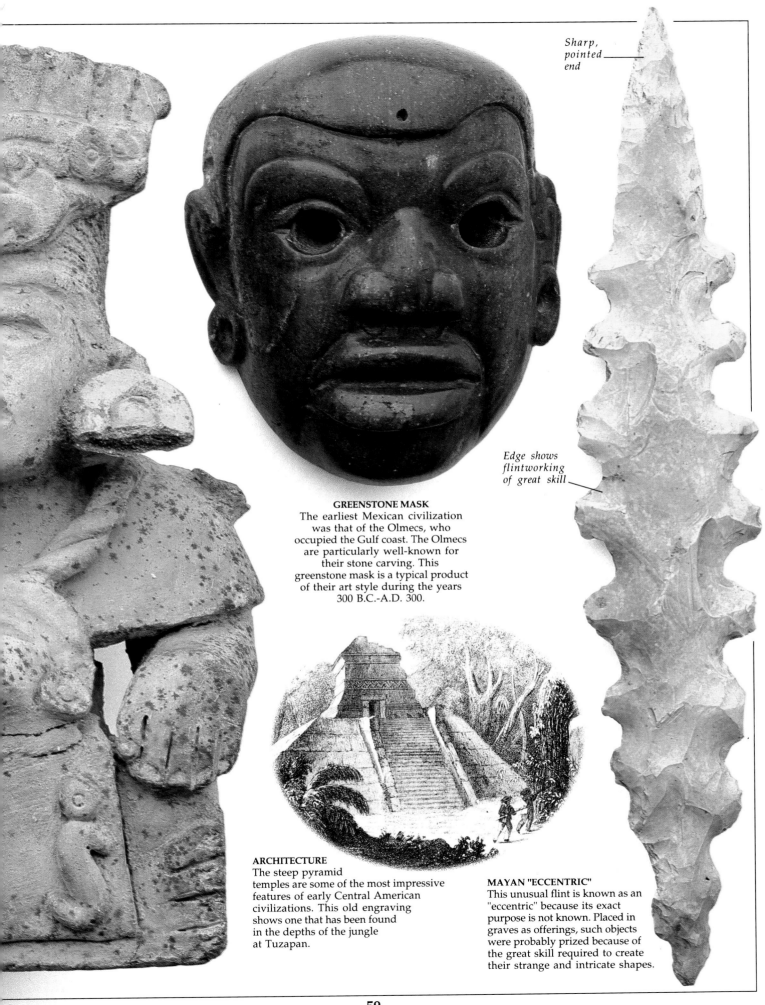

Sharp,
pointed
end

GREENSTONE MASK
The earliest Mexican civilization
was that of the Olmecs, who
occupied the Gulf coast. The Olmecs
are particularly well-known for
their stone carving. This
greenstone mask is a typical product
of their art style during the years
300 B.C.-A.D. 300.

Edge shows
flintworking
of great skill

ARCHITECTURE
The steep pyramid
temples are some of the most impressive
features of early Central American
civilizations. This old engraving
shows one that has been found
in the depths of the jungle
at Tuzapan.

MAYAN "ECCENTRIC"
This unusual flint is known as an
"eccentric" because its exact
purpose is not known. Placed in
graves as offerings, such objects
were probably prized because of
the great skill required to create
their strange and intricate shapes.

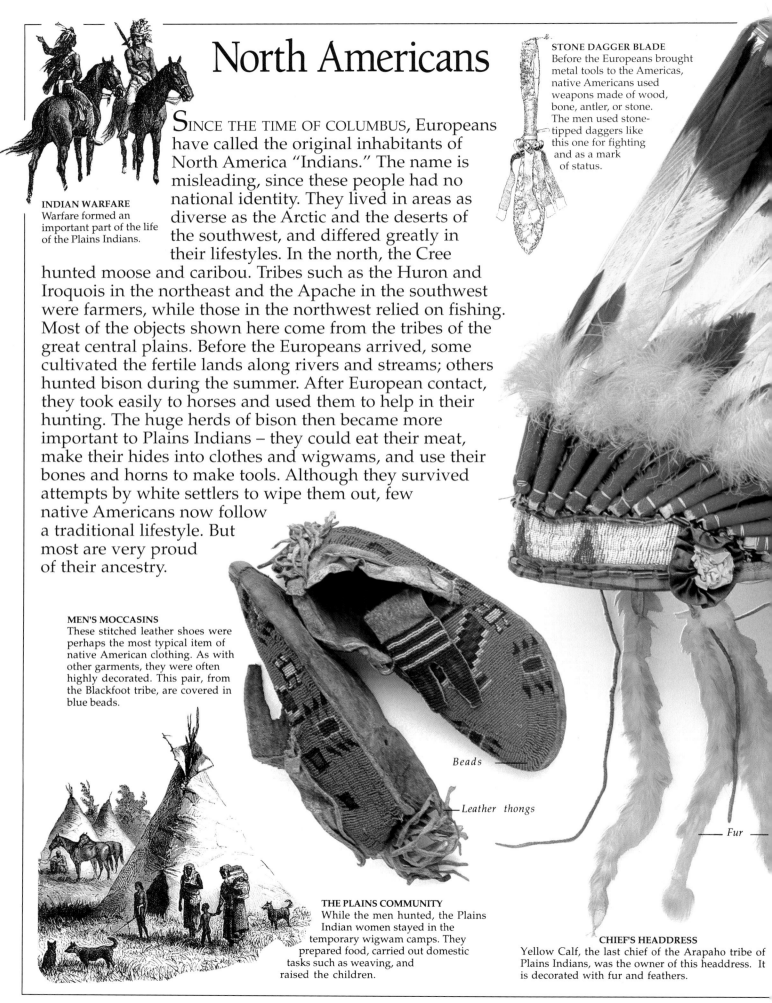

North Americans

SINCE THE TIME OF COLUMBUS, Europeans have called the original inhabitants of North America "Indians." The name is misleading, since these people had no national identity. They lived in areas as diverse as the Arctic and the deserts of the southwest, and differed greatly in their lifestyles. In the north, the Cree hunted moose and caribou. Tribes such as the Huron and Iroquois in the northeast and the Apache in the southwest were farmers, while those in the northwest relied on fishing. Most of the objects shown here come from the tribes of the great central plains. Before the Europeans arrived, some cultivated the fertile lands along rivers and streams; others hunted bison during the summer. After European contact, they took easily to horses and used them to help in their hunting. The huge herds of bison then became more important to Plains Indians – they could eat their meat, make their hides into clothes and wigwams, and use their bones and horns to make tools. Although they survived attempts by white settlers to wipe them out, few native Americans now follow a traditional lifestyle. But most are very proud of their ancestry.

INDIAN WARFARE
Warfare formed an important part of the life of the Plains Indians.

STONE DAGGER BLADE
Before the Europeans brought metal tools to the Americas, native Americans used weapons made of wood, bone, antler, or stone. The men used stone-tipped daggers like this one for fighting and as a mark of status.

MEN'S MOCCASINS
These stitched leather shoes were perhaps the most typical item of native American clothing. As with other garments, they were often highly decorated. This pair, from the Blackfoot tribe, are covered in blue beads.

Beads

Leather thongs

Fur

THE PLAINS COMMUNITY
While the men hunted, the Plains Indian women stayed in the temporary wigwam camps. They prepared food, carried out domestic tasks such as weaving, and raised the children.

CHIEF'S HEADDRESS
Yellow Calf, the last chief of the Arapaho tribe of Plains Indians, was the owner of this headdress. It is decorated with fur and feathers.

SCRAPING TOOL
Hides were prepared
by scraping them
with a metal-bladed,
bone-handled tool.
Earlier peoples used
flints in a similar way.

Horsehair

PAINTED HIDE
This animal hide is
decorated with colored ink
drawings of warriors mounted on
horseback attacking bowmen with
spears. The horsemen are wearing
long feather headdresses. This
hide is about 6 ft (2 m) long. It
belonged to a group of Sioux or Crow
Indians.

*Feathers indicate
success in hunting
and war*

EARTH LODGE
Some tribes built their homes by
constructing a roof over a deep
pit. This illustration shows
such a dwelling - a Mandan
earth lodge - in the nine-
teenth century.

Digging up the past

ARCHAEOLOGY PROVIDES our only means of studying most early people, as written records have only been available for a fraction of our time on earth. Modern archaeology is a far cry from its old image of hunting for treasure in lost cities. Today the archaeologist employs a whole battery of scientific techniques to help detect, excavate, and analyze the remains of ancient societies. He or she is most likely to be interested in small pieces of pottery or fragments of insects, plants, or animals, because of the information these can give about everyday life. Although archaeology is often thought of as excavation, the story only begins there. Once a "dig" is over a great deal of time is spent analyzing the material recovered, and preparing it for publication. When it is published, the notes, finds, and samples are displayed or stored in a museum.

WORKING ON SITE
Unlike the careless treasure-hunting of the past, modern excavation involves the meticulous vertical and horizontal recording of all features of a site. This is the excavation of an early hominid in Sterkfontein, South Africa.

PHOTOGRAPHIC SCALES
Photographs form a vital part of the records of an excavation. These scales are essential for judging the size of the subject being photographed.

CAST OF THOUSANDS
Giovanni Belzoni was one of the first to bring Egyptian relics to the West. However, he was a shameless treasure hunter who also destroyed much important material.

Trowel

Small, solid-forged steel blade

Paintbrush

Toothbrush

Cotton gloves

CLEANING
For items needing careful cleaning on site, a variety of instruments, such as these brushes, might be used.

Metric scales

TROWEL AND GLOVES
The trowel is the main tool used for excavation. Gloves may be used to handle delicate finds after digging.

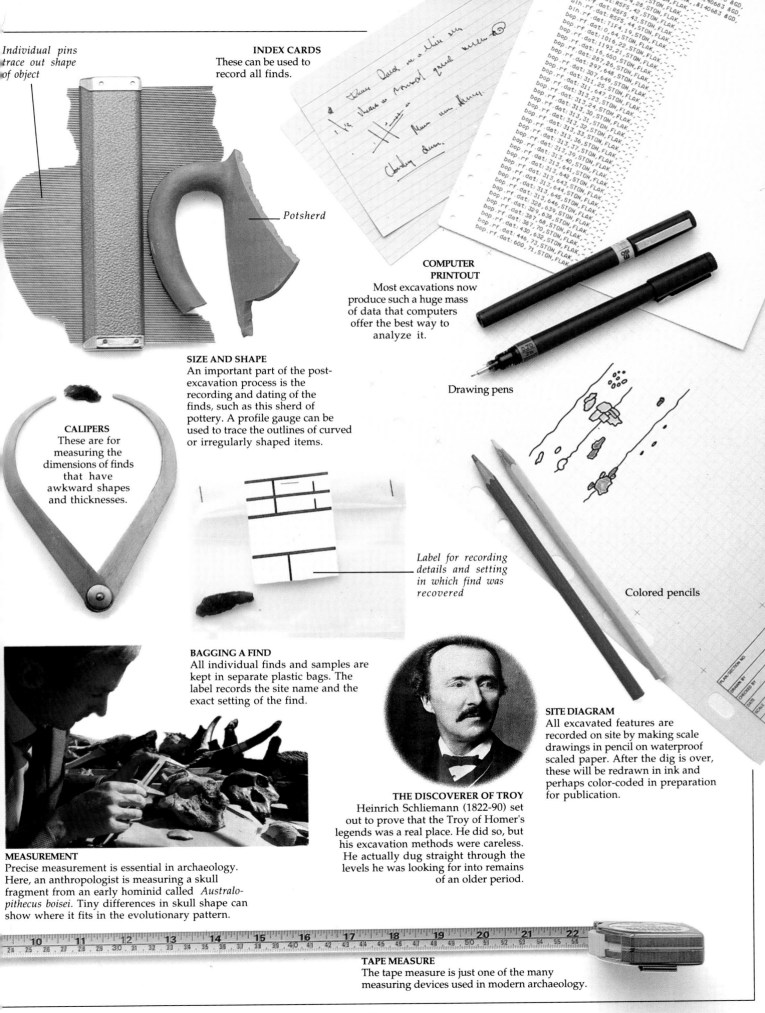

Individual pins trace out shape of object

INDEX CARDS
These can be used to record all finds.

Potsherd

COMPUTER PRINTOUT
Most excavations now produce such a huge mass of data that computers offer the best way to analyze it.

Drawing pens

SIZE AND SHAPE
An important part of the post-excavation process is the recording and dating of the finds, such as this sherd of pottery. A profile gauge can be used to trace the outlines of curved or irregularly shaped items.

CALIPERS
These are for measuring the dimensions of finds that have awkward shapes and thicknesses.

Label for recording details and setting in which find was recovered

Colored pencils

BAGGING A FIND
All individual finds and samples are kept in separate plastic bags. The label records the site name and the exact setting of the find.

SITE DIAGRAM
All excavated features are recorded on site by making scale drawings in pencil on waterproof scaled paper. After the dig is over, these will be redrawn in ink and perhaps color-coded in preparation for publication.

THE DISCOVERER OF TROY
Heinrich Schliemann (1822-90) set out to prove that the Troy of Homer's legends was a real place. He did so, but his excavation methods were careless. He actually dug straight through the levels he was looking for into remains of an older period.

MEASUREMENT
Precise measurement is essential in archaeology. Here, an anthropologist is measuring a skull fragment from an early hominid called *Australopithecus boisei*. Tiny differences in skull shape can show where it fits in the evolutionary pattern.

TAPE MEASURE
The tape measure is just one of the many measuring devices used in modern archaeology.

Did you know?

Nabta megaliths, Egypt

The Nabta megaliths were recently discovered in the Egyptian Sahara. The circle of stones is astronomically aligned, although no one is sure of its exact purpose. It dates to between 4500 and 4000 BCE – making it 1,000 years older than the circle at Stonehenge in Wiltshire, England.

Czech anthropologists have found Ice Age clay fragments that show impressions of clothes worn by women 25,000 years ago. Rather than wrapping up in furs and hides, it seems likely that women wove their own textiles, using plant fibers. Experts think that Ice Age outfits included skirts, belts, and bandeaux (cloth wound around the upper body).

The Maya were drinking hot chocolate as long as 2,600 years ago. Scientists have found cocoa residue in a spouted pot discovered at Colha, Belize. The Maya liked unusual flavorings in their cocoa drinks – corn, honey, and even chili pepper!

Evidence of two early hominids was found in a cave in South Africa in 2000. The jaw and skull belong to a male and female *Australopithecus robustus*, who lived 1.5 to 2 million years ago. The fossils were found close together, as if they were kissing. They have been nicknamed Orpheus and Eurydice, after a pair of mythical Greek lovers.

In 1998, remains were found in Portugal of a boy who had both Neanderthal and Cro-Magnon features. The 24,500-year-old skeleton was found near Leiria, north of Lisbon. It was the first evidence that the two human species interbred. That means that some Neanderthal genes may survive in modern Europeans.

The Stone Age is sometimes called the "Acheulean age." The term comes from the village of Saint-Acheul in northern France. It was here that amateur archaeologist Jacques Boucher De Perthes discovered flint hand axes and other Ice Age tools in the 1830s. At the time, the idea of a Stone Age culture was almost unbelievable, and went against the teachings of the Church.

Cro-Magnons are named after a cave in the Dordogne, France. In the 1860s, French geologist Louis Lartet found skeletons of prehistoric people there. The bones belonged to *Homo sapiens* and were between 10,000 and 35,000 years old.

Until recently, scientists thought that *Homo erectus* disappeared around 200,000 years ago. However, fossil finds suggest that *Homo erectus* may have survived on Java until 50,000 years ago, which means the species might have been present at the same time as *Homo sapiens*.

The earliest evidence of trepanning is the 7,000-year-old fossilized skeleton of a man found at Ensisheim, in Alsace, France. He had two holes in the skull. One had completely healed; the other, which was a massive eight square inches (57 square cm), had only partially healed.

Ruins of a Neolithic house at Skara Brae

Skara Brae is a Neolithic village on Mainland, one of the Orkney Islands in Scotland. It lay buried under sand for 4,350 years until a storm revealed it in 1851. Even the furniture in the huts was made from stone slabs – then, as now, few trees grew on Orkney.

Experts argue about exactly when the dog became man's best friend. Wild wolves probably began to hang around human settlements from 15,000 years ago. These animals gradually became smaller and more at ease with people. They acted as guard dogs and helped early people hunt. In return, they received leftover scraps of food.

Wolf

Record Breakers

OLDEST SPEARS
The earliest known specialized hunting weapons are the four 400,000-year-old spears found in 1997 at Schoeningen, Germany.

OLDEST TOOL USER
The jaw of an early human was discovered at Hadar, Ethiopia, in 1994, near stone tools. Dated to around 2.33 mya, it is the earliest find of tools and human bones together.

EARLIEST MUSICAL INSTRUMENT
In 1995 a Neanderthal flute, made from the leg bone of a bear, was discovered in a cave near Idrija in Slovenia. It was 45,000 years old and had four different notes.

LARGEST MOUNDS
One of the Cahokia Mounds in Illinois is nearly 100 ft (30 m) high and 975 ft (300 m) long. In England, Sudbury Hill is 130 ft (40 m) high, and covers 5 acres (2 ha).

OLDEST TATTOOS
A 5,300-year-old "iceman," discovered frozen in the Alps, was found to have 57 tattoos in various places on his body.

QUESTIONS AND ANSWERS

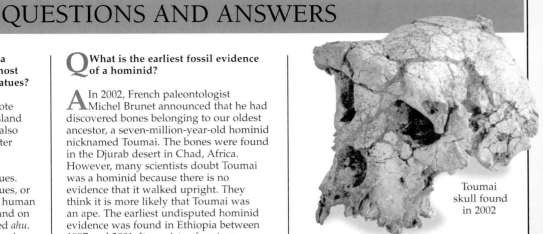

Toumai skull found in 2002

Q What area has the most prehistoric statues?

A The remote Pacific island of Rapa Nui, also known as Easter Island, boasts hundreds of prehistoric statues. Most of the statues, or *moai*, are huge human figures that stand on platforms called *ahu*. They were carved between CE 1000 and 1500. Experts think that at least 800 of the statues were made and that they probably represented ancestor gods. The remains of 400 can still be seen in and around the island's quarry, Rano Raraku. One unfinished statue is over 66 ft (20 m) long. It has been christened "El Gigante" and would have weighed as much as 270 tons. All that is known about the culture that produced the statues is that a handful of Polynesian seafarers colonized the island around CE 400 and that, by the time European explorers discovered the island in the 1700s, the population was in decline.

One of the Easter Island statues

Q Who was the Iceman?

A "Otzi" is probably the world's most famous ice mummy, and also one of the oldest, dating back 5,200 years. The body of this 40-year-old Stone Age man was discovered by two German hikers on the border of Austria and Italy in 1991. Along with Otzi's frozen corpse there were more than 70 objects, including a copper ax, a flint dagger, a bow, arrows, and a quiver – the personal belongings he was carrying when he died. There are no signs that Otzi was killed in a ritual sacrifice, like some ice mummies. It looks as though he was caught in a freak snowstorm, high in the mountains, and starved or froze to death. Thanks to the freezing conditions, even Otzi's clothing has been beautifully preserved. He was wearing a grass cape and special snowshoes that had thick bearskin soles. Several tattoos were found on Otzi's body, positioned over swollen arthritic joints. Experts think that tattooing may have been used as a kind of magic charm, to cure the pains of arthritis.

A careful examination of the remains of Otzi the Iceman

Q What is the earliest fossil evidence of a hominid?

A In 2002, French paleontologist Michel Brunet announced that he had discovered bones belonging to our oldest ancestor, a seven-million-year-old hominid nicknamed Toumai. The bones were found in the Djurab desert in Chad, Africa. However, many scientists doubt Toumai was a hominid because there is no evidence that it walked upright. They think it is more likely that Toumai was an ape. The earliest undisputed hominid evidence was found in Ethiopia between 1997 and 2001. It consists of various bones belonging to *Ardipithecus ramidus*, a hominid that lived between 5.2 and 5.8 million years ago.

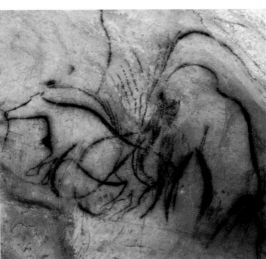

Stone Age rock art, discovered on a cave wall in France

Q Who was nicknamed the "Father of Prehistory"?

A French priest Henri Breuil (1877–1961) is known as the Father of Prehistory because he dedicated his life to the study of prehistoric cave art. In 1901 he found paintings at Combarelles and Font-de-Gaume in the Dordogne. He went on to become an authority in the field, writing more than 600 articles and books. He was one of the first people to see the paintings found at Lascaux in 1940, and also discovered evidence that humans had lived in the caves.

Q Where are the world's oldest cave paintings?

A The world's oldest paintings were discovered at Chauvet-Pont-d'Arc, in the Ardèche region of France in 1994. Three cave-explorers – Jean-Marie Chauvet, Eliette Brunel, and Christian Hillaire – discovered the paintings in a network of chambers set into the cliffs. The Chauvet paintings were made around 31,000 years ago, earlier than any other cave art discovered so far. They show hundreds of figures, including 47 rhinos, 36 lions, and several bears. It seems likely that the cave art was religious in some way, perhaps depicting important myths.

Q Could Neanderthals talk?

A Scientists cannot agree on whether Neanderthals could talk. Some believe that their skulls show evidence of muscles that could precisely control their tongues, and that Neanderthals could have spoken, probably in very deep voices. They argue that Neanderthals must have had language in order to pass on skills such as tool making. Other scientists remain unconvinced. They think that it was the Neanderthals' lack of language that put them at such a disadvantage when modern humans arrived on the scene.

Who's who?

NEW FOSSIL DISCOVERIES add to our knowledge of early hominids all the time. Each new find, australopithecine or human, moves scientists a step closer to creating an accurate picture and chronology of our ancestors.

AUSTRALOPITHECUS AFARENSIS

3.8–3.0 MILLION YEARS AGO (MYA)

LUCY'S CLAN
Most of our knowledge of *Australopithecus afarensis* is based on the "Lucy" skeleton found at Hadar, Ethiopia. The species was smaller than modern humans – about 3 feet 3 inches (1 m) tall – but their hips and limbs suggest that they walked upright.

AUSTRALOPITHECUS BOISEI

2.3–1.2 MYA

ROBUST VEGETARIAN
Unlike *afarensis*, *boisei* belongs to the group of "robust" australopithecines that had sturdier skulls and larger teeth. *Australopithecus boisei* may have used their large molars for grinding through a vegetarian diet.

AUSTRALOPITHECUS AFRICANUS

3.0–2.0 MYA

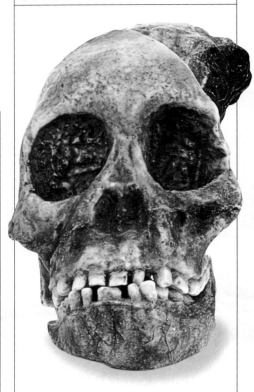

THE TAUNG CHILD
Australopithecus africanus was about the same height and build as Lucy. Most evidence is based on a child's skull (above) from Taung, South Africa. Holes in the skull suggest the Taung child was killed by an eagle.

HOMO SAPIENS

0.1 MYA–PRESENT

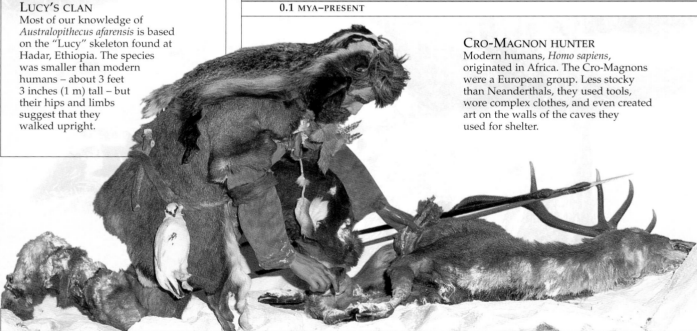

CRO-MAGNON HUNTER
Modern humans, *Homo sapiens*, originated in Africa. The Cro-Magnons were a European group. Less stocky than Neanderthals, they used tools, wore complex clothes, and even created art on the walls of the caves they used for shelter.

HOMO NEANDERTHALENSIS

120,000–30,000 YEARS AGO

BIG-BRAINED HOMINIDS
Neanderthals were shorter than modern humans, with adult men reaching about 5 feet 6 inches (1.7 m) tall. However, they had larger brains than modern humans. With stocky bodies, they were well adapted to their Ice Age environment, and they may have worn clothes, too.

HOMO ERECTUS

1.6–0.2 MYA

OUT OF AFRICA
Homo erectus ("upright person") was present in the Far East from about 1.6 mya. Fossils found on the remote Southeast Asian island of Flores suggest that *Homo erectus* built boats and traveled across the seas.

HOMO ERGASTER

1.9–1.2 MYA

GRASSLANDS HUNTER
The best-known *ergaster* (work person) is the "Turkana boy" skeleton, found in Kenya. Fleet of foot, *ergaster* lived in the savanna, hunting animals for food and killing them with simple stone tools.

HOMO HABILIS

2.4–1.6 MYA

HANDYMAN
One of the earliest *Homo* species, *habilis* used stone tools and may even have been capable of primitive speech. About 4 feet 6 inches (1.5 m) tall, they had larger brains than the australopithecines, but were still quite apelike in appearance.

Find out more

Hut reconstructed using original stones

THERE ARE MANY ways that you can find out more about our earliest ancestors. Books are a good source of information, and there is lots of useful data on the Internet as well. Also look for television documentaries about excavations, prehistory, or early civilizations. Museums are full of interesting ancient artifacts; visit them to see human skulls, reconstructions, and items such as clothes, tools, and figurines. Finally, in some areas there is evidence set down in the landscape itself, in the form of ancient mounds and standing stones.

Animal hide

IRON AGE HUTS, PORTUGAL
If you are lucky enough to go to northern Portugal, visit Citania de Briteiros – a large Celtic hill settlement not far from the city of Braga. The site includes the ruins of more than 150 stone huts, a few of which have been rebuilt. The region was once a Celtic stronghold, and the ancient city was still active when Portugal became part of the Roman Empire.

STONE AGE CAPERS
The movie *The Flintstones* (1994), inspired by the popular cartoon, offered a humorous look at the Stone Age. Of course, movies like this say more about our modern world and technologies than they do about the past – but that doesn't stop them from being entertaining.

USEFUL WEB SITES

- Origins of Humankind site with reviews, news, and links:
  www.versiontech.com/origins
- Human Evolution site, with timelines and hominid descriptions:
  emuseum.mnsu.edu/biology/humanevolution/index.shtml
- British Museum collections from Prehistory and Early Europe:
  www.thebritishmuseum.ac.uk/pee/peehome.html
- The Hudson Museum, with fascinating online exhibits:
  www.umaine.edu/hudsonmuseum/
- The official site for the Lascaux cave paintings:
  www.culture.fr/culture/arcnat/lascaux/en/

MENHIRS IN CARNAC, FRANCE
At Carnac, in southern Brittany, you can see more than 3,000 ancient monuments, arranged in circles and avenues. Most are upright standing stones, or menhirs. Stone Age tribes erected them 6,000 years ago. Over the years, many fell over, but in the 1930s a local enthusiast, Zacharie Le Rouzic, started a campaign to restore them to their original positions.

These menhir are made of granite

AN AERIAL VIEW

The remains of Old Sarum hill fort near Salisbury, in Wiltshire, can be seen best from the air. The outer defensive walls probably date back to the Bronze Age, around 1000 BCE In the Iron Age, the inner rampart was constructed. The settlement was later used by the Romans, who renamed it Sorviodunum, and later still by the Saxons, Danes, and Normans.

Mammoth's flesh preserved in the icy Siberian tundra

MAMMOTH DISCOVERIES

We know from finds in the Russian Ukraine that *Homo sapiens* sometimes used mammoth bones as a framework for their animal-skin tents. The photo above shows the first major discovery of a complete mammoth. Its 44,000-year-old corpse was found on the bank of the River Berezovka, Siberia, in 1900. The mammoth skeleton can still be seen today, on display at the museum of the Zoological Institute in St. Petersburg, Russia.

Decorative studs of opaque red glass

THE BATTERSEA SHIELD

You can see this Iron Age shield, which was found in the River Thames, on display in the British Museum. It dates to between 350 and 50 BC. Made from a thin sheet of bronze and measuring just 1 ft (78 cm) long, it would not have afforded much protection in battle. It is more likely that it was a ceremonial shield, possibly thrown into the river as an offering to the gods.

Celtic-style motifs of circles, spirals, and S shapes

Places to visit

AMERICAN MUSEUM OF NATURAL HISTORY, NEW YORK, NEW YORK
(212) 313-7278
www.amnh.org
The Hall of Human Biology and Evolution has life-size dioramas of *Australopithecus afarensis*, *Homo eraster*, Neanderthals, and Cro-Magnons. There are also replicas of Ice Age art from the Dordogne and full-size casts of Lucy and Turkana Boy.

NATIONAL MUSEUM OF NATURAL HISTORY, WASHINGTON, D.C.
(202) 633-1000
www.mnh.si.edu
A re-created Neanderthal burial site, stone tools, and ancient artwork tell the story of early man. On the Web site, visit the Human Origins Program to see a Human Family Tree, information on new research, and the Ask a Researcher program.

SAN DIEGO MUSEUM OF MAN, SAN DIEGO, CALIFORNIA
(619) 239-2001
www.museumofman.org
Exhibits on ancient Egypt, the Maya, and California's own Kumeyaay bring anthropology to life. Guided tours and workshops are offered.

SERPENT MOUND STATE MEMORIAL PEEBLES, OHIO
(513) 587-2796
Serpent Mound, built between 800 BCE and CE 1, is an embankment that resembles a snake. A quarte of a mile long, it is the largest serpent effigy in North America.

BRITISH MUSEUM, LONDON
One of the world's most famous museums, the British Museum has rooms full of objects relating to early people and civilizations, including pottery, precious grave goods, and ancient weapons. It recently opened a new gallery that is dedicated to prehistoric finds.

Glossary

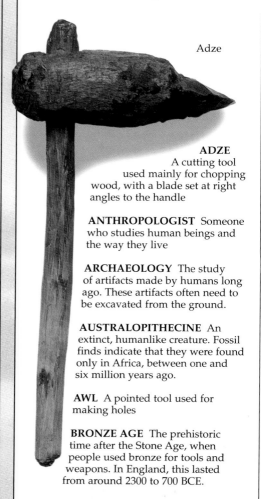

Adze

ADZE A cutting tool used mainly for chopping wood, with a blade set at right angles to the handle

ANTHROPOLOGIST Someone who studies human beings and the way they live

ARCHAEOLOGY The study of artifacts made by humans long ago. These artifacts often need to be excavated from the ground.

AUSTRALOPITHECINE An extinct, humanlike creature. Fossil finds indicate that they were found only in Africa, between one and six million years ago.

AWL A pointed tool used for making holes

BRONZE AGE The prehistoric time after the Stone Age, when people used bronze for tools and weapons. In England, this lasted from around 2300 to 700 BCE.

CELTIC Relating to the Celts, a group of Iron Age farmers who lived across northern Europe

CIVILIZATION A settled society that has developed writing, trade, organized religion, architecture, and a form of government

CLIMATE The average weather of a place over a period of time

CRO-MAGNON The name given to an early type of *Homo sapiens* that lived in Europe in the Stone Age and produced spectacular cave paintings

CULTIVATE To grow plants as crops

CUNEIFORM The first written language, invented by the Sumerians around 8000 BCE

CURE To treat meat or an animal hide so that it will not decompose

DEMOTIC A popular and efficient form of writing used by the ancient Egyptians

DIVINING Using magic to find out about the future and other mysteries

DOLMEN Prehistoric stone structure, where two or more erect stones support a "table top" made of one large, flat stone

ETHNOGRAPHY The study of the different human races

EVOLUTION The process by which species change into new ones, occuring gradually as some characteristics are kept and others are lost or modified

EXTINCT Describes an animal or plant species that has died out

FIRE DRILL A primitive fire-making device, incorporating a stick that is twirled to create friction – and a spark

FLINT A type of stone that chips in a way that produces sharp edges; frequently mined in prehistoric times and used for simple tools

FOSSIL The naturally preserved remains of animals or plants, or evidence of them

FRESCO A wall painting

GEOLOGIST Someone who studies rocks

HALBERD An axlike weapon with a long shaft

HIERATIC SCRIPT A simplified version of hieroglyphs, used by the ancient Egyptians

HIEROGLYPHS Picture writing used in ancient Egyptian script

HILL FORT A prehistoric stronghold, built either on a naturally occurring hill or on a mound made by people

Egyptian hieroglyphs

HOMINID A member of the family *Hominidae*, which includes our apelike ancestors, such as australopithecines, as well as *Homo neanderthalis* and modern humans

HUNTER-GATHERER Someone who survives by hunting animals and gathering wild plants for food

ICE AGE The Pleistocene Epoch, which lasted from two million to 15,000 years ago, or one of the cold snaps during that time, when ice sheets spread out

A dolmen at Comenda, Portugal

IRON AGE The prehistoric time after the Bronze Age, when people used iron tools and weapons. In England, the Iron Age began around 700 BCE.

KAYAK A sealskin canoe used by the Inuit

KOHL Black powder used to create dramatic eye makeup

MEGALITH A prehistoric monument consisting of one or more huge stones

MUMMIFICATION The process of preserving a body so that it will not decay

Megaliths at Carnac, France

NEANDERTHAL An extinct hominid of the species *Homo neanderthalis* that lived in Europe and the Middle East from 120,000 to 30,000 years ago. The name comes from the place in Germany where the first Neanderthal fossils were found.

NEOLITHIC The New Stone Age, which began around the time of the last Ice Age. Neolithic people used more complex stone tools, built stone structures, and began to make pottery.

ORE Rock from which metal is extracted

The Great Pyramid at Giza, Egypt

PALEOLITHIC The Old Stone Age, when people first used simple stone tools. It began around two million years ago and lasted until around the time of the last Ice Age.

PALEONTOLOGY The study of fossils

PAPYRUS An early form of paper used by the ancient Egyptians, made from pulped stems of a river reed of the same name

PIGMENT The chemicals that give something its coloring. Early cave artists used pigments made from plants and minerals.

PREHISTORY The time before there were written records

PYRAMID A massive stone structure with a square base and sloping sides; usually either a royal tomb or sacrificial temple

QUERN A stone mill, used for grinding grain such as corn

RELIEF Artwork, such as carving, that stands out from its surface

SMELTING Melting ore to separate out the metal

SPECIES A group of animals or plants that share characteristics and can interbreed. *Afarensis* and *africanus* are both species of australopithecine.

STONE AGE The prehistoric time before the Bronze Age, when people used tools and weapons of stone. The Stone Age is split into two main periods, the Paleolithic and the Neolithic.

TECHNOLOGY The practical uses of human knowledge, referring both to skills and the creation and use of new tools. New technology is driven by new discoveries and new uses for old knowledge.

TORC A twisted metal band worn as a necklace or bracelet

TREPANNING Cutting a hole in the skull; a type of surgery performed in prehistoric times, perhaps to free evil spirits

TUNDRA Land around the Arctic where the ground is frozen all year round and trees cannot grow

Stone Age carving from Ulster History Park, Omagh, Northern Ireland

Chumash Painted Cave, California, where Chumash Indians used pigments to create religious artworks

Index

Acknowledgments

The publisher would like to thank:
Peter Bailey and Lester Cheeseman for additional design assistance; Angela Murphy for additional picture research; Dr. Schulyer Jones, Julia Cousins, Ray, Inskeep, John Todd, and John Simmonds of the Pitt-Rivers Museum, Oxford; Dr. David Phillipson of the University Museum of Archaeology and Anthropology, Cambridge; Gavin Morgan of the Museum of London; Colin Keates and Chris Stringer of the Natural History Museum; the staff of the Museum of Mankind; Dave King and Jonathan Buckley; Meryl Silbert.

The following museums provided objects for photography:
British Museum (Natural History) 6–7, 10–11, 14–15, 18–19, 22–23
Museum of London 26–27, 30–31, 32–33, 46–47, 52–53, 62–63
Museum of Mankind 20–21, 38–39, 60–61
Pitt-Rivers Museum, Oxford 12–13, 16–17, 28–29, 34–35, 36–37, 56–57
University Museum of Archaeology and Anthropology, Cambridge 24–25, 40–41, 42–43, 44–45, 48–49, 50–51, 54–55, 58–59

Picture credits:
(t=top, b=bottom, c=center, l=left, r=right)

Agence France Presse: 65tr.
American Museum of Natural History: 18b, 67tl, 67br.
Bridgeman Art Library: 62lc.
British Museum (Natural History): 6r,

15bl, 19bc.
Bruce Coleman: 7bc, 10l, 62tr, 63br.
Corbis: /Jason Hawkes 69tr; /Jon Sparks 64tl.
Tim Daly: 66–67.
Alistair Duncan: 70–71, 71tr.
Heritage Image Partnership/The British Museum 69c.
Kobal Collection: *The Flintstones in Viva Rock Vegas* © Amblin/Univ/Hanna-Barbera/Michaels, Darren 68cl.
Mansell Collection: 8cl, 9br, 13c, 17tr, 27bc, 33tl, 36tc, 41rc, 42tl, 43rc, 46lc.
Mary Evans Picture Library: 9tr, 16tl, 20tr, 21bc, 22br, 25br, 26tl, 30lc, 31br, 32br, 35c, 41rt, 42c, 51br, 52rc, 53tl, 54c.
Angela Murphy: 7bl, 23cl.
Museum of London: 24bc, 25tl, 47c, 48bl.
Peter Newark's Historical Pictures: 24tl, 25cl, 28tc, 34tl, 41bc, 49br, 60tl, 60br, 61br.
Rex Features: Olympia/SIPA 65b.

Ronald Sheridan's Photo Library: 22tr, 38tl, 50tl, 55r, 63br.
Topham Picture Library: 10bl.
Torquay Museum: 66b.
University of Colorado at Boulder: Professor J. McKim Malville 64tr.
Alan Williams: 71br.

Illustrators:
John Woodcock
John James
Mark Bergin

Jacket credits:
Front: Tl: Julia Margaret Cameron/© Bettmann/CORBIS; Tcl: Pitt Rivers Museum, UK; B: © Gianni Dagli Orti/CORBIS. *Back:* Museum of London (cl, tr); Museum of Mankind (c); Pitt Rivers Museum (cb, r); University Museum of Archaeology and Anthropology, Cambridge (bl).